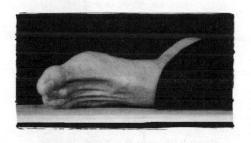

# FOOTNOTES*

## * a memoir

# TOMMY TUNE

simon & schuster

SIMON & SCHUSTER
Rockefeller Center
1230 Avenue of the Americas
New York, NY 10020

SIMON & SCHUSTER and colophon are registered
trademarks of Simon & Schuster Inc.

Designed by Amy Hill

Manufactured in the United States of America

ISBN 0-684-84182-7

✶ "Every memory is self-serving, and the occasional admission of error offers the author an opportunity to congratulate himself for his honesty and courage in mentioning it."

—*John Gregory Dunne*

*The Witch.          *The Bitch.

*I never had a grandfather; one was crushed in a coal mine collapse when Mom was four, and the other, after "another hopeless day on the farm," killed all his hired hands, shot Grandma, and then himself. She lived, he died. So I was left with two grandmothers—one was a witch and one was a bitch. I *loved* the witch.

People from miles around would come in horse-drawn buckboards to collect her and her "divining rod," driving her off to their Oklahoma pastures, and she'd tell them where to drill the well. She was a "water" witch with 99 percent accuracy. She also had the county's only "madstone," so if your child "got bit" by a rabid dog, you'd bring the little fella to "Old Miz Tune." She'd draw the madstone out of the buttermilk in which it always soaked and, with strips of cloth, bind it to the bite. Poison sucked out, child lives, madstone back in the buttermilk. But enough of this background stuff, let's talk about Broadway!

* It was St. Patrick's Day nineteen sixtysomething when I arrived in Manhattan, driven up from Texas by the guy who probably loves me and show business more than any guy I've ever known: Phillip Oesterman. Phillip said, "In Houston if you dance, are talented, and extremely unusual they call you a sissy or a weirdo. In New York they call you a star. You're comin' with me." And off he drove me in his Ford Fairlane to New York City.

Stopping on the corner of Fifth Avenue and 50th Street on that warm day in March he said, "See that newsstand, Tune? Buy yourself a copy of *Backstage* and a copy of *Show Business* and see what's auditioning." Well, among others, there was an audition for *Irma La Douce* starring Genevieve. I loved Genevieve. I'd watched her on *The Jack Paar Show*, which was *the* talk show of that era. Between him and Steve Allen, the talk show medium was born—God help us—and in those days talk shows were really good, or at least *brand new*. Famous stars and eccentric talkers would guest with Jack Paar, and the conversations were hilarious and compelling. Genevieve was my favorite guest, and I always read up on *TV Guide* so that I never missed an appearance. Apparently she was a poor little Parisienne who had a tiny one-room café on the Left Bank where she cooked, served, and entertained. What an adorable young woman she was, with her sexy accent and her pixie hairdo. One night she gave herself a haircut right on the show! Well, come on, what do you want? I knew what I wanted. I wanted to marry Genevieve.

So, the audition for *Irma La Douce* was at 2:00 P.M., Showcase Studios, Seventh Avenue and 56th Street. First New York audition, first day in the big city, and I got the job! Now, that's a success story, all right, and except for one week spent as a concept coder for Young & Rubicam, I've been able to support myself in my chosen field ever since. I've danced in the chorus, I've danced in front of the chorus, I've choreographed Broadway shows, and I've directed Broadway shows. I've had a career in the theater, and I've always paid my bills. I'm so lucky.

*Irma La Douce* had a cast of seventeen men and one woman, and we traveled the country, playing the Lenny-Debin circuit—which was all in tents—and later moving inside into real theaters like the Coconut Grove Playhouse in Florida, the Papermill Playhouse in New Jersey, and the John Kenley theaters in Ohio.

Genny loved to drink, as did everyone in those days, as I remember, and every night after the show we certainly did. One night in Millburn, New Jersey, after one too many "Patriot Cocktails" (Applejack, lemon juice and Cointreau), we got a bit rowdy. I remember Gabe

Dell flopping his dick out on his dinner plate and garnishing it with parsley—"Hors d'oeuvres, anyone?" It made Genny laugh so hard she peed. Some locals objected to our behavior and rightly so. A punch-up ensued, and the next thing I remember is the entire company in the Millburn courthouse standing in a long line at drunken attention in front of a very *sober* judge.

Genny played Joan of Arc to the max, "But your 'onor—dey are joost young men 'aving a leetle joie de vivre in your beautiful village." He wasn't having it, and it looked like we were gonna spend the night in the clinker. Through my haze at the end of the line I saw a door. Let's talk dancing. You know that magic step where your toes meet each other and then you swivel to where your heels meet each other and voilà! you have magically moved to your right one whole foot? You've seen it in all my shows. I love that step. My mother taught it to me. It's a Charleston step. Well, I started doing it, in what I remember as slow motion, toward the door. Arriving, I slowly opened it and kept doing the same magic step till I had disappeared—all six feet six and a half inches of me. How could they not have seen me? In the dark, down some stairs, I fumbled, found a door leading outside, and stumbled into the back of a cast member's van where I promptly passed out.

The next morning after a night in jail, with a record to prove it, the entire cast was released, all worried about what had happened to its youngest member. There I was, a free man, asleep in the parking lot.

There was one Black member in the cast, an absolutely beautiful dancer who played the role of Persil, le Noire. His name was Judd, and I was amazed by his physical perfection. I'd never known a Black person before, coming from the seriously segregated South, and I was completely fascinated with him—how he spoke, how he acted. He was so at ease and confident and so different from the Black people I had observed down home in Houston. I'd had a Mammy named Evalina whom I loved, and I'd overheard Black people talking to each other in the back of the bus; but there was not one Black student in my entire high school, and I'd never, never had a conversation with one in an equal forum. On a rehearsal break we went to the coffee shop in the Edison Hotel—nowadays it's called the Polish Tea Room by Broadwayites—and sat down at the same table, and nobody cared or stared or threw him out or called me names for associating with him. Down home they would have yelled "nigger-lover"; not so at the Polish Tea Room. This was brand new. This was taboo. This New York City nonjudgmental attitude seemed so free and so sophisticated for this Texas hick. My heart beat really fast. I'm sure my eyes bugged out. I was short of breath. I was excited. So no wonder later in the tour on that drunken night in Warren, Ohio, when he came a knockin' on my hotel room door after the show . . .

Am I moving too fast with this story? It's so telling when you finally sit down to write what you remember, the order in which it comes to you. They say everybody has a book in them—or at least a made-for-TV movie. Well, they also say, "If wishes were biscuits we'd *all* eat." Actually, *they* didn't say that—my mother always said that, and then she'd dance away into the kitchen singing, "I'm always chasing rainbows—watching clouds drifting by. . . ."

Mother was a flapper—a definitive flapper—and piecing together the stories she told me, it's clear she must have been quite "madcap." Here's one: This is in the twenties, and the local movie house in Shawnee, Oklahoma, was having a talent contest before the movie screening. The sign read: FREE DISHES AND MONEY PRIZES, quite a lure for a family of three brothers, one sister, no father, and a hard-working mother. Mom and her girlfriend Bobbi Pratt put together a Charleston act—I know it was good because Mom could really dance—in which she played the boy and Bobbi played the girl. Mom had secretly borrowed her youngest brother's new outfit—"Norfolk" jacket and knickers, knee socks, oxfords, and a matching cap—Bobbi wore fringe, and they won the contest.

Now, Mom's mother (the bitch) was sitting in the first row of the balcony, enjoying the show, not knowing that her only daughter was a contestant. But she did recognize the suit, and mentally scolded her youngest son for loaning it to that fellow down there on the stage "cuttin'-a-rug." Lo and behold the winners were announced, and as they came out for a bow, Bobbi—that "scamp of a vamp"—took off Mom's cap as she bowed and down

＊Mom on wheels with kickstand.

*Mom and me.

tumbled Mom's beautiful dark hair. The jig is up: "That's no fella, that's my daughter!" The prize was withdrawn by the judges, citing fraud. Mom's brother was furious since he had never even worn the suit yet himself, and my mother's aborted debut on the "Great American Stage" was in drag, which is why I'm in a little bit of trouble today!

★ I have one tiny photograph of Grandpa Tune. He was tall and thin and looks exactly like Sam Elliot, the movie actor. In this photo, he is wearing bib overalls—a striking, raw-boned farm boy. My Dad, however, was a mountain of a man, two hundred and fifty pounds at least—thick wrists, size seventeen collar, and hands like the Michelangelo *David* (huge and always perfectly manicured). He was always impeccably dressed in handsome ties, hand-tailored shirts from the Thomas Shirt Company of Oklahoma City, custom-made suits, shined shoes, and snap-brimmed felt Fedoras.

"Dad, when am I gonna fill out?" I would ask.
"Don't worry, I was a beanpole like you till I
    was fifteen."

Well Dad, I'm still waiting. The only full thing I inherited from my Dad were his lips. And his feet. We have identical feet—extremely high arches—except I'm one size bigger. I used to be able to wear his cowboy boots, but then too many years of tap dancing took their toll and I don't fit into them anymore. Too bad, he had quite a collection.

Dad was always whistlin' and whittlin' and dancin' with Mom whether in the kitchen, in the living room, or in the den. In fact, they met dancing at an Oklahoma City hop. He asked her to dance, she said yes, and here I am. At a wedding party at the Shamrock Hotel in Houston when I was about nine, I saw them really dance together, with all the trappings: the Henry Bussey Orchestra; a shiny, spacious dance floor; a mirrored ball, Mom in a swank teal blue dress and (always) high heels. "I can't walk in flats," she'd say, and I never saw her in flats—never. Even her house slippers had heels.

Oh, how they danced that wedding night. As the other couples were pushing and pulling each other around the floor, my parents seemed to glide above the masses. Dad, huge but weightless, like a balloon (Daddy gave new meaning to the phrase "light on your feet"), and Mom, thin, tall but looking petite in Dad's arms as he guided her through the clumsy crowd. They moved effortlessly—she following his every lead—not a misplaced step. Amazing. Two moving as one.

*I was crucially embarrassed.* I could hardly watch— what were they doing? Why weren't they doing it like everyone else? Then slowly, couple by couple, avenues formed, providing space for them, and then finally the

*With Dad on the front porch.

*Mom and Dad when hats were in.

whole floor cleared. Everyone just watched them. Good Lord, what was happening? They floated together in the open space. To my young eyes it was shockingly intimate, but I was no longer embarrassed. They were doing it differently than the rest of the lot, but clearly they were doing it the best. They were like The Old Smoothies, that once famous ice-dancing team, only Mom and Dad didn't need the ice. They were smooth without it. The tune finished. The whole ballroom applauded. Wow!

I guess I was born to dance. It's in my blood—their blood. Years later when I danced with Mom I was amazed at her ability to follow my every move. I'm not a very good partner. I can teach someone the choreography and we can dance together, but just taking a partner onto the floor and leading them in an improvised pattern is not my forte. However, Mom could follow the slightest nod of a lead and had this skill of becoming magically weightless in your arms, and you were free to dance without the slightest encumbrance. It was almost like dancing by yourself, only with a partner attached, which somehow made it more astonishing, better. I've always thought that two was a better number than one. "People go for pairs in a big way," said Charley Baxter, a street entertainer I played in *Busker Alley*, a new musical that never made it to Broadway. More on that subject later.

At a Tony Award Ball one year—I'd won for something—I danced with Donna McKechnie, and I experienced the exact same feeling as dancing with Mom that I just described to you. That amazing ability to let go and float—Donna was the same, the *same*. Anywhere I wanted to go—through, around, dip, slide, twirl, hesitate, on—not a missed step by Donna, just like Mom. I couldn't believe it. It scared me. It was so intimate.

* I think the very few times I've been fortunate enough to experience true intimacy with another human being have been quite frightening to me. I love it at the moment it's happening, crave it when I remember it, and the urge for a repeat performance returns, but inevitably I find a way to flee from it, lest it become available as a way of life. Too powerful for me, it is. I experience a sense of drowning. I suppose that's why some of my most momentarily successful romances have been with married people. With them I have the unspoken safety-net line—"But you're married"—thus keeping me from being swallowed up in a sea of intimacy. As much as I yearn for a personal attachment, that's how much I fear it. I *really* want a marriage and I *really* don't, I reckon, because surely by this time in my life—and I'm fifty-seven as I write this—I could have had it. Maybe I just got off on the wrong foot. Like a show with an opening number you can't get right, the launch is everything. I

usually do umpteen versions of the opening number for a show I'm directing. It's so important to set the tone for the evening, to define the rules from which the audience can sense the strange world they're going to inhabit for the next two hours. I say strange world because it truly is if you dissect it. Just consider how the house lights seem to "brown-out" and no one panics; a large velvety curtain mysteriously rises, seemingly of its own accord; a large group of musicians led by a man with a stick strikes up harmonies and rhythms from a vast pit in front of the stage; people in costumes and makeup in impossibly bright lights enter and speak louder than necessary and act like we're not watching them, then when they can't shout anymore at each other they start singing as if this were a natural thing to do, and then when they can't sing anymore they start to dance uninhibitedly. The number comes to a halt—we, the audience, clap as the artists stand there in tableau, panting; the applause dies, and the troupe continues its story like nothing has happened. Giant painted trees and rocks slide offstage as a golden staircase whirls onstage; a window unit backed by a snow-covered vista flies in apparently from heaven, and we sit there accepting this foolishness; and if we're lucky we believe it, and we laugh and cry with the characters and are entertained and enlightened. When it works, time passes in an instant, we're transported, and we leave the proceedings enriched for the rest of our lives. That's musical theater. However, it all begins with the opening number. At the beginning of an evening in the theater you've got to seduce them into your arms, into the whole.

That's what happened to me with my first sexual experience. I was seduced into her arms and more than that. Even though I was in college I was unbelievably naive for my age. In fact, I've always been about ten years behind in my development as a human being, not just with sex, but with my whole experience of living. I suppose that's why I always feel like I'm getting in on the "tail end" of things. I got to Hollywood in time to appear in the last big movie musical, *Hello, Dolly!*, starring Barbra Streisand and directed by Gene Kelly—his last, Hollywood's last. Then on to television for *The Dean Martin Show*, working as an assistant choreographer—the last days of the television musical variety show. My nightclub act with the Manhattan Rhythm Kings, after being held over for two weeks, literally closed the beautiful Venetian Room of the Fairmont Hotel in San Francisco, a good finale for that famous room that had showcased the talents of Tony Bennett, Ella Fitzgerald, Peggy Lee, Lena Horne, Joel Grey—all the great nightclub entertainers of that time. There are no more rooms like that anymore. Today, I've reached what appears to be the end of Broadway, as every year fewer and fewer successful new musicals are being written and mounted on the Great White Way. The tail end.

But I mean to be writing about beginnings here. Sexual beginnings. Here goes.

She was a teacher in East Texas, where I attended ju-

*With The Manhattan Rhythm Kings.
We toured our act all over the world from
Monte Carlo to Moscow.

nior college my freshman year. She was theatrical, attractive, unusual, a good talker, leggy, and married. After one of our dance concerts in a neighboring town she drove me back to her home—it was late and campus was a long distance—and put me in her son's room. He was spending the night at a friend's house. Her husband was asleep in the master bedroom. Actually, "passed out" would be a more apt description, for he was a drunkard, but a cheerful one, and seemed sort of like a coach—athletic, trim, energetic, red-faced. He was, of course, an alcoholic, but we didn't know that word in those days. Anyway he was "out like Lottie's eye," as Mom used to say, and I was asleep in Buster's room, when suddenly I felt her presence beside me. We had never verbally acknowledged the attraction we had for each other, but that didn't mean it wasn't happening—and holy smokes, here she was!

"What about your husband?" I whispered.
"Oh, he's out for the night," she said.

Not knowing where to put it or what to do with it, and wanting but also not wanting to flee, I ventured, "I don't want to hurt you." I'd heard that line in a movie once and remembered it. Well, it happened. Wow. Fireworks. Mushi-wushi. Yum yum. Safe and warm and hot and dangerous. I thought, "Be quiet, Tommy, don't make noise, her husband's in the next room. Uh-oh. This smells really hot." Pow. Eruptions. Afterward she whispered, "You don't have to worry about hurting me," and the secret affair had begun. It lasted till I went to the University of Texas, and I don't *think* anyone on campus ever knew. To this day, I remember she had the smoothest inner thighs I've ever experienced.

She came to visit me the next winter at the university, but it was all different. *She* was different, slightly heavier and not as much fun. We quarreled, about what I don't know. I slipped and fell on the ice, and she cackled like a witch. Why was she laughing at me? I could have broken something. Maybe I had. Her heart. Our bond. Later, I got a letter from her telling me that she had miscarried our child but not to worry about her, the only loss was the child itself. How's that for an opening number? Hell, we're just getting started here.

And how did I get started? Dancing. I got started dancing.

I remember that a dance teacher came around every so often to our elementary school and taught us a few basic moves. I could learn 'em and do 'em, so she called my parents and told 'em she thought I had talent. They thought it was a ruse to get more students in her dancing school, but when I asked how much it would cost, she answered, "Gratis." I looked it up—it meant free. Dancing boys were rare. Off I went to dance class. Does this sound like a monologue from *A Chorus Line*? Of course it does; it *is*.

I started in a class with all boys. Thirty minutes of tap, thirty minutes of tumbling. I was so skinny that

*My first dancing recital, as a dormouse (tumbling) and in white tails (tapping).

Mom sewed little pillows inside my dance clothes so the tumbling wouldn't bruise my bones. In my first appearance on stage I was one of sixteen dormice (tumbling) and one of sixteen candy canes (tapping). I was the littlest one in class so I was on the end of the line. For the tap number we wore white tailcoats with red-and-white-striped linings. On our long flap-ball-change exit, the little boy in front of me was such a slowpoke I wanted to give him a shot of ginger in his butt. I pushed him instead, and the audience laughed and clapped.

I didn't realize it was me they were reacting to till Mom told me afterward. She was laughing and saying that she would have done the same thing to give him a little "gumption." "Honey, he was slowin' up the works. Everybody clapped for you 'cause you took up the slack." I guess I've been trying to take up the slack on-stage ever since.

That was on the stage of the Music Hall in Houston, Texas. It was the spring recital of the Emmamae Horn School of Dance. She was my first dancing teacher, and she had great taste and a fertile imagination and remains a huge inspiration. In fact those "dogies" in the opening number of *The Will Rogers Follies* were a steal from Emmamae's spring recital of 1947. Her routine was set to "The Cow Cow Boogie," and the costumes, faux cowhide bodysuits with longhorns and rope tails, are almost identical to our Broadway versions. In New York at the *Follies* I was vilified by the feminists for those costumes. ("Women as meat? Mr. Tune, how could you?") It's all a

⋆ In New York with Emmamae Horn as she was honored by
the Dance Masters of America. After I presented her
with the Award, she whispered in my ear, "Let's bow" and
she effected a deep and graceful curtsey. Emmamae
taught me how to put on a show.

little Texas dancing teacher's fault for inspiring me to make fun shows. Thank you, Emmamae Horn.

Emmamae and her husband Jesse lived a block away from our house. I was simply in love with her, and I'd hide behind the bushes to watch her do her gardening—in pink ballet slippers with pink ribbons crisscrossed around her ankles. She knew how to put on a show, and when dancing school shut down for those long hot Houston summers I'd get the neighborhood kids together and direct miniversions of her recitals that we performed in the backyard. We charged two cents, but the lemonade was free. I didn't know about concessions then.

It was at one of these performances that I lost trust in my father. I had told him how I needed a curtain and a wire to hold it up. It was to be made of burlap, and I was convinced the show couldn't flow properly without it. He promised he'd get it made out at the shop. Dad, the farm boy, had made his way in the oil fields of Oklahoma and Texas as a roughneck and was now the owner of the L&H Machine Works, which serviced Wilson Drilling Rigs. They had all this machinery in the plant, and I believed him when he said he could effect the curtain and poles that I needed. I remember checking with him as the big day approached. His vagueness didn't worry me; he'd get it done.

The show day arrived, and the audience was assembling in Martha and Betsy's backyard—no sign of a curtain. We waited, with me anxiously running out back behind the garage to look for his green Pontiac. I kept telling the kids that I was sure he'd be arriving at any minute. Mom finally said we should start, and we did. The curtain never came and neither did Dad. I was really let down. The show was just awful without the curtain, and I was crushed. I secretly never again depended on Dad to keep his word, and I suppose that was the beginning of my making shows that don't depend on scenery to be successful. I've favored basically blank stages or unit sets throughout my directorial career, and it most likely dates back to this early scenic disappointment.

Decades later I had another huge scenic disappointment in the making of a Broadway show, *Grand Hotel: The Musical*. The only set piece was a large and beautiful revolving door of glass and bronze that could manually be moved about the stage by an enormously strong uniformed doorman. The finale of *Grand Hotel* as I conceived it was this: The revolving door was to be positioned very far downstage—close to the audience—as the entire cast created an "infinity" pattern, "figure eighting" and reweaving in and out of the door as a grand opera drape, depicting the exterior of the Grand Hotel with all the myriad windows aglow, descended. Slowly, like the house curtain at the Royal Opera House at Covent Garden or the Met, the "drape" would symmetrically lower from each side of the proscenium opening, pausing for an instant to frame just the revolving door and then—silently in one final whoosh—closing, shutting off the interior of the Grand Hotel, leaving us, the audience, outsiders, peering in through the lighted windows at a bygone elegance. Following was a slow fade to darkness as the orchestral vamp subsided. Magic.

Well, it just wouldn't work. The curtain refused to meet in the middle properly. The elegant draped closing that I envisioned was lopsided, askew, pitiful, a non-effect. Finally the two pieces were sewn together as one, and the slow curtain came from above in the "guillotine" fashion, cutting off the heads, the bodies, and finally the feet of the intertwining characters. The split second the drop intersected with the stage floor, the lights in the windows came on. It was effective. It was not what I wanted. It took me back to the show in the backyard in Houston. Well, at least I had a *curtain*, which was more than Dad came up with. I never let on to him how disappointed I was. It was a secret hurt. I wonder how many more I harbor within me. Oh well, it was just a show, not brain surgery.

My second year at dance school was a big surprise. All the other little boys had dropped out, and I was put in a class of all girls; we were taught thirty minutes of tap and thirty minutes of ballet. Well, I loved ballet—the sensation of flying—and even though it hurt, it didn't hurt half as much as my bones had from banging the floor in tumbling class. Shortly thereafter, Aunt Eunice took me to see the Ballet Russe de Monte Carlo, which played a split week at Christmastime in Houston. There on the Music Hall stage was this colorful world of beau-

*My second dance recital. My partner, Patricia Swanzey, was taller than me and really pretty. Our routine, which included a pantomime, was set to "Strolling Through the Park One Day" blending into "And the Band Played On." Mom made all my costumes expertly. The jacket was rose taffeta and the pants were green and white polished cotton. Neat.

tiful people in elaborate costumes telling stories of passion and romance and fantasy without using a single word, just movement. *Scheherazade, Swan Lake, Don Quixote Pas de Deux*—I was entranced. It was also, as I remember, very sexy. I had no idea why I was so fascinated, but I was.

Aunt Eunice wasn't really my aunt, but down home in Houston children were taught to address all adults as "Aunt" Vera, or "Uncle" Jiggs, instead of "Mr." or "Mrs." Murray. It was confusing to have so many aunts and uncles but that's the way it worked. I heard Aunt Eunice after the ballet tell someone on the phone, "Those queer sons of bitches stuff socks in their jockey straps. What a sight they make leaping about the stage in their tights." What a sight indeed!

Then (American) Ballet Theatre came to town, and Aunt Eunice took me to see that too—*Billy the Kid, Lilac Garden, A Streetcar Named Desire, Graduation Ball, Interplay*—I was hooked. Back to ballet class I went with new-found fervor and dedication. Spring recital that year we did *Les Sylphides in Miniature*, and I padded my part but not my tights. In fact I remember Mom telling me to "rearrange yourself, you're poochin' out" as she wrinkled up her nose like it was something distasteful. I did my best not to "pooch out," since volume between the legs was obviously not desirable. I meant to tell Aunt Eunice that they weren't jockey straps we wore. They were dance belts, and they were really uncomfortable up the crack. Nowadays, however, thanks to Calvin Klein underwear ads, we "pooch out" all we want. Things change, but dance belts remain uncomfortable.

✳ The lighting at the ballet was always so fascinating to me. It appeared to come predominantly from both sides of the stage, not from overhead or from the front. I remember the followspots from the projection booth, of course—those beams shooting out through the darkness above our heads and landing on the most important dancers on stage—but that low side lighting that seemed to imitate the Texas sunsets held my eyes fascinated. I knew the geography of the Music Hall quite well from our spring recitals, so after one performance of Ballet Theatre, I used the pass door, audience right to nip back and get a look at those side lights and ran smack dab into the leading dancer John Kriza on the stairwell. He scared me to death. He had on so much makeup he looked like a mannequin. Thick black eyebrows, orange grease paint, lined lips, and dark shading beneath the jawline—he had looked so devastatingly handsome a few minutes earlier from out front, and here we were face to face and he looked like a horror show. I fled, but not before I got a peek at those side lights. They were so bright. How could the dancers make those leaping and turning and running exits di-

*The Tunes going to see Paul Draper dance at the Music Hall in Houston. He performed The Rhapsody in Blue wearing a gray turtleneck, gray slacks, and gray tap shoes—monochromatic magic. A tap ballet. Nobody did it like Paul Draper. I was transfixed. So was Dad. He loved watching tap dancers. Maybe that's why I became one.

rectly into the wings while being blinded by those brilliant lights? Years later I learned that the low sidelights are called "shin busters," and I'm sure they've lived up to their name.

As beautiful as the onstage world appears to the audience, that's how dark and perilous backstage is. Dangerous. Treacherous. Most accidents occur in the wings, not onstage where you're only walking the tightrope. Backstage is a highwire act. A gaggle of electrical cables, ropes, stored sets, sharply changing floor levels, uneven footing, ramps, lighting instruments, and overhead pipes—all to be navigated in the dark so no worklight can spill onto the stage and ruin an effect. Caution!

In the early eighties when I was appearing in *My One and Only* at the St. James Theatre in New York there was no behind-the-scenes crossover on stage level so I had to go downstairs under the stage using the basement as passage to get from stage left to stage right. Low-hanging pipes downstairs were a hazard to someone of my height, and too many times in my life I have forgotten how tall I am and bang! I have a veritable mountain range of bumps on my cranium that I've accumulated throughout the years. I don't clear most doorways, but I'm used to stooping through them; it's all the other low-hanging potential disasters that you gotta watch out for. On good weather nights I used an unusual passage to get back to stage left. There was a pass door to West 44th Street stage right at the St. James, and if I hotfooted it, I could dash outside, cross under the marquee in front of the theater, slip up the stage door alley in past "Pops," and there I was stage left for my next entrance. This didn't work when it was raining and snowing but it sure saved that bent-over run I had to make through the basement most nights. One evening, making this mad dash under the marquee I ran smack dab into Carol Channing. She was startled to see me, and I think to this day she believes I'd run out of my theater just to say hello—right there on 44th Street in full makeup and costume. How unprofessional would that be!

Since she's made her entrance into this story I suppose it's time to write about her. Carol Channing is my theatrical godmother. I met her when I was nineteen, dancing chorus in the Dallas Summer Musicals where I got my Equity card. We had just finished *West Side Story*, a really first-class production, and we were in rehearsal for *Redhead*. *Show Girl*, her revue, was playing the interim week, and what a *Show Girl* she was. I'd never seen anything like her before—statuesque, every feature larger than life—shucks, she was Texas-size and had the ability to give us a closeup while we watched from the back row. I was hooked from the start. I watched every performance, entranced. She did a wicked impression of Marlene Dietrich that had us rolling in the aisles with laughter; she was so hip as she explained the Broadway musical through history. What an informative entertainment it was, filtered through her wide-eyed and tilted sensibilities. Then came the

*In *West Side Story*. That's me
seated in the middle of the gang.
God, what an actor!

curtain speech wherein she referred to the cavernous State Fair auditorium as a "monument!" Every time she said "monument" she spread her arms wide and tilted her torso to the left. Her speech was riddled with subtext, which was always what made Carol Channing great. There's so much more going on inside her than meets the eye. The hair and makeup and physicality are all smoke screens covering the wickedly witty depths of this woman. Liz Smith calls her a "closet intellectual," and she's right.

Through the years I've gotten to spend valuable time with Carol Channing and with her husband, Charles Lowe, who makes it possible for her to go about Caroling the world. Once she was comfortable in acknowledging my respect and devotion to her, she started giving me advice, which I've always followed.

"Tommy Tune, go on tour with this show [*My One and Only*]. You must play the capitals of the world."
"Name one."
"Ah . . . MinneAAApolis."

And her critiques of shows in preview are equally valuable. After seeing *The Best Little Whorehouse Goes Public*, my first big musical flop, she said, "Tommy Tune, it's the musical of the future." See? She knew it wasn't for *now*. And after seeing a particularly poor performance of *Busker Alley* in Costa Mesa she ventured, "Tommy Tune, I liked the 'sex tap' but the rest of the show is a downer." She was right. She told me: "The Lunts convinced me to *tour* if I wanted a career in the theater. Then those people will come to see you on Broadway because you've already come to see them in *their* town. It's like they *know* you, that's how it works." Carol Channing knows.

So, there I was on tour in San Francisco with *My One and Only*, and unbeknownst to me it was my one thousandth performance of the show. All through that evening I kept seeing these little specks of red confetti on the stage. A dancer has to constantly survey the terrain he's negotiating each night because it changes, and one is constantly at peril. A piece of a showgirl's costume has fallen off—an earring, a bobby pin, a water puddle that hasn't dried from a preshow mopping—all these things are potential disasters for a dancer. But this particular night it was all these little red dots of confetti. "What's this all about?" I complained to myself as I danced through my routines. "Damn." Here's what it was about.

I'm taking my curtain call and hear the audience erupt suddenly, and there, through a snowstorm of red confetti falling from the flies, all in white chiffon with wings stretched out like an angel, comes Carol Channing, San Francisco's own Carol Channing, presenting me with her own Diamond Award—"It's been given to many famous women, Lady Bird Johnson, Jacqueline Kennedy Onassis, Golda Meir—it's true that diamonds are a girl's best friend, but I've never

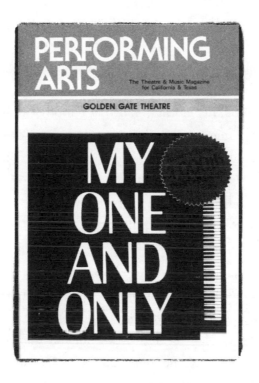

*It happened in San Francisco at the Golden Gate Theatre. The Shorensteins, who own the theater, made my thousandth performance into a milestone memory.

known a man to turn one down!" (laughter) "Whereas," she read from the Mayor's proclamation, "Tommy Tune is making his 1,000th performance in this great Broadway hit in our city and whereas, . . . well you know how these things are—they go on and on and on, but anyway the Mayor's just crazy for Tommy Tune and it's my honor to introduce the person who made it all possible—the person without whom there would be no Tommy Tune—all the way from Texas here's Little Missus Tune, his mother." Through another downfall of confetti comes Mom—what a surprise—dressed in bright red and looking so great and she's saying to me through the applause, "Why is she callin' me little— I'm not so little."

"I know Mom, you're tall, it's just a term of endearment."

What a night! Gold stickers had secretly been put on all the *Playbill*s stating, "This is Tommy Tune's 1,000th performance of *My One and Only*." So the whole audience knew, the whole cast and crew, but not me. So, who's counting? Anyway one thousand seems like *bupkis* when you align it to Carol Channing's record with *Hello, Dolly!*

What a creation Carol Channing is! Nobody talks, or walks, or looks like her unless they're imitating her. She is unique. Born for the stage. What a blessing she is to the theater! What an inspiration!

I have a lot more to say about my theatrical Godmother, but I'll drop it in later. A little of the Carol Channing vitamin goes a long way.

\* 1,000 and counting. Charles "Honi" Coles,
Lucie Arnaz, me, and Carol Channing,
hugging "Little Missus Tune."
Red confetti everywhere.

Thinking about that run in San Francisco of *My One and Only* brings something else to mind. I was playing opposite Lucie Arnaz by then. Having opened on Broadway with Twiggy to enormous success, with Sandy Duncan replacing her, and then Lucie, the show and all of its words and moves had taken on an almost mythical quality by now. In other words it was *set*, and it worked like gangbusters. There was a lot of dancing in the show, a lot of singing, a lot of jokes, and a lot of kissing, so you must imagine my shock when at "half hour" before a Saturday night performance Lucie comes into my dressing room and announces, "I can't kiss you anymore—so I'll keep my lips pressed together like this (*a stony pursing of the mouth*) and place them here (*somewhere in the vicinity of my left nostril*), and we'll turn upstage so the audience can't tell."

Dumbfounded, I asked, "What? Do you have a cold? I'm not worried. I never catch colds. I never get sick."

"No," she said, "I don't have a cold—but you might have AIDS."

I was stunned. "Why would you think that?"

"It's just that Larry (her husband) has been talking to doctors and they told him that you can get it from kissing, and so I'm not gonna kiss you anymore. . . ."

"But Lucie," I said, "we kiss twenty times during the show. I kissed you twenty times at the matinee today. If you don't want to kiss me anymore, OK—but we have to work this out in rehearsal. We can't just go for the nose

*My "Four" and Only. I played the show with Twiggy, Sandy Duncan, Lucie Arnaz, and Stephanie Zimbalist. I cherish long runs. To do the same show, night after night, always heading toward perfection, is a privilege.

and turn our backs out there tonight—and what about the necking scene in the car—how do we turn around for that?"

In a panic she responded, "I can't help it, I can't kiss you again," and she left.

"Places" announced the stage manager. I felt contaminated, judged, guilty, hurt, shocked, puzzled, and worse, underrehearsed! Well, the show that night was so clumsy, and this incident colored the rest of the tour for me.

It put a hold on our long-term loving relationship. I'd known Lucie since she was seventeen. We'd met on *The Dean Martin Show* when we created a number called "The Name's the Same" in which all these offspring of famous parents appeared: Francesca Hilton (daughter of Zsa Zsa Gabor and Nicky Hilton), Meredith MacRae (daughter of Gordon and Sheila), Maureen Reagan (daughter of Ronald and Jane Wyman), Lucie, Desi Jr., Gail Martin (Dean's daughter), etc. Years later I was present for Lucie's first ever Broadway audition. She'd flown in seeking the role of Gittel Mosca in the national tour of *Seesaw*. She was so nervous that her voice shook, and we thought she had a permanent motor in her vocal cords. But once we calmed her down, she was able to sing the score, and her acting, although invulnerable at the time, shone bright and smart. She got the role, and we had one of the great times of our lives, those nine months on the road with *Seesaw*.

I was playing the role I'd created a stir with on Broadway in 1973—David, a gay choreographer looking for his Broadway break. I had been nominated for a Tony, and during our Boston run I flew in to New York for the Tony Awards ceremony—national TV, celebrity presenters—just like the Oscars but for the theater. Holy smokes!

Going into the Shubert Theatre that "Tony night," I shook hands with Paul Newman at the door—the producer, Alex Cohen, had coerced him into being the official greeter. I heard a husky voice behind me say, "Beautiful as ever." I turned around and was face to face with Melina Mercouri, a white ostrich feather boa around her throat, dark eyes blazing, a mane of hair— she was present, really present. I repeated her words back to her, "Beautiful as ever," and she radiated!

I'd been warned by Michael Bennett, my mentor, to take a *girl* to the ceremony. How could I do that to Michel Stuart? He'd seen me through the whole nine yards, even to the point of getting me costumed for the role in a way that really worked for me. Ann Roth was the costumer of *Seesaw* and, with Lainie Kazan's firing and Michele Lee's hiring and all the out-of-town woes we encountered getting *Seesaw* to Broadway, she welcomed Michel's input. Having shared my life for several years, he'd come to really understand what I looked good in and what I didn't. He had an amazing eye for line, for design, for life. I owe Michel Stuart so much. He really was a great awakener in my life. It's sort of like B.C. and A.D. I was one person before I met Michel Stuart (B.M.S.) and another person after I met him (A.M.S.) I owe so much to the people who have loved me, and I want to give so much to the people I love. Unfortunately, they're not always the same people.

Anyway, going against Michael Bennett's stern advice, "Have a girl on your arm even if it's Pat Ast!" Michel Stuart and I inched our way into the Shubert Theatre—the tall nominee and his boyfriend. We were seated on the last row—me on the aisle, then a support column between us, then Michel's seat, so if the TV camera should need to land on me, you the viewer wouldn't see that I didn't have a girl date. For those years, I suppose coming with Michel Stuart as my date was radical behavior. Suzanne Pleshette was the presenter of the Best Featured Actor in a Musical category. Dutifully reading the crawl she said, "This category has quite an impressive history of former winners: Yul Brynner, Tom Bosley, Harry Belafonte. The nominees are . . ." As each nominee was named, the TV camera picked up their faces in the audience, and we saw them on the monitors in the auditorium. When she said my name the camera stayed on *her*. Wow, I thought, something must have gone wrong. Then she announced, "And the winner is—Tommy Tune for *Seesaw*."

The orchestra played the Cy Coleman-composed *Seesaw* theme and down the aisle I trod. The camera *had* to be on me now, and I made the only good acceptance

speech I've ever made, because it was the first. Afterward Michel Stuart thought it was "too much," but
years later, in a montage of acceptance speeches shown
on the Tony telecast, my speech was included, and I
wasn't embarrassed at all. It was from the heart and it
was generous, and it was young and excited and somehow very pure and sincere. As Sonja Gibson says, "I'm
always sincere, whether I mean it or not!" Well, I meant
it. I walked off stage and Bette Midler and Liza Minnelli
were standing there in the wings to congratulate me.
Was this a dream? No, I had arrived, but there was still
that odd thing about the TV camera not picking me up
in my seat—was it because of Michel Stuart? I've
thought about this a lot, and I've decided the answer is,
*yes*, because of Michel Stuart. In my ears, the wise,
stern words of my mentor are still ringing, "Have a girl
on your arm, even if it's Pat Ast!"

Back to Boston with my trophy in tow—out on the
stage for the first performance as a Tony Award winner.
Huge applause. Boston, at that time, was a big town for
theatergoers, and they'd all seen the Tony telecast the
previous evening. I was radiating like Melina Mercouri
by now. I did my big dance, stopped the show, went into
the choreographed exit, and fell down. Humility, Tommy,
humility. "Hemorrhoids," as Joel Grey's ex-wife used to
say, "are one of God's little levelers." So is falling down.
Humility, Tommy, humility.

Well, in spite of falling down in front of everyone, I
thought I was pretty hot stuff and remained thus for the

rest of the *Seesaw* tour. Not until I returned to New York, unemployed, did reality set in. You mean I'm not a star? You mean everyone doesn't want me to sing and dance and act on their stage? What do you mean I'm not the right type? Go with the talent! I've got credentials. Nothing. *Nada, Niente, Ne pas rien.* Well, *now* what?

Lucie had decided to take up residence in New York after the *Seesaw* tour to seek her career on Broadway. We were very close then. Nothing much, after our great success across the country with *Seesaw*, was happening for her either. Michel Stuart said if I wanted a professional performing career I would have to get married. "Why not marry Lucie," he suggested.

"Marry her? We haven't even fornicated!" Again that uneasy feeling of not being legitimate, and Michael Bennett's voice, "Have a girl on your arm, even if it's Pat Ast!" More on that feeling later.

I return now, many years later, to the onstage kissing problem with the *My One and Only* tour and Lucie Arnaz. I hope you're not confused. My life is one long tour, and we're in the eighties now. What terror there was in those early days of AIDS. What terror there still is. Anyway we worked it out choreographically so it wasn't too obvious that the romantic leads in *My One and Only* didn't kiss each other anymore, but it wasn't any good. The chorus kids, watching from the wings, noticed and discussed it in their dressing rooms, and then looked away. A curtain had fallen between Lucie

*Unemployed in New York
after the *Seesaw* tour. My
career isn't smokin' but I am.
Which way now?

and me. I was an untouchable. "Does she know something I don't know?" I wondered. "Do I have AIDS?" There wasn't a real test in those days so I felt like my life was on hold. Standing ovations and rave reviews, and another Tony Award, this time for Best Actor in a Musical for *My One and Only*. Success and emptiness. I didn't want to touch anyone or be touched. We ended up not speaking to each other. Then came the closing performance of the tour—I, of course, didn't even know what city we were in by now, but our contracts had been completed. In our final performance on stage after she sings "How Long Has This Been Going On?" to me and we come together, me in my groomsuit and her as the beautiful bride—final clinch, fake kiss—she puts her mouth on mine and pries my lips open with her tongue—a "soul kiss," I believe is the expression—long and sloppy. And I'm thinking, "We're behind in the music—we're supposed to be walking off into the sunset by now," but we just stood there kissing and crying, and the curtain fell.

We've never mentioned this—Lucie and me—and we're close friends again and neither of us has AIDS. Pull the scrim. Turn the page. Life goes on, if you're lucky, and I'm so lucky.

*Together again with Lucie.
Time heals everything.

✳ The first time I got drunk I was four years old. It was at a Christmas party on McClendon Street in Houston and all the adults were drinking "Super Dupers," a mixture of bourbon, Dubonnet, Coke, and half a lemon served in a huge iced tea glass with lots of cubes. Delicious. I kept traveling from aunt to uncle and back for little sips. Presently I was in the middle of the floor dancing and stumbling about, and everybody was laughing and clapping. I was the center of attention and loving it. "Uh oh, the mule throwed Tommy!" Laughter. "Uh oh, the mule throwed Tommy." I was drunk.

I heard my parents say to others, "We always encourage our kids to drink at home so when they go out on their own they'll know how to handle it." "Our kids" were my two sisters and me. All exactly ten years apart. I wonder if my parents did it only once every decade. Not possible, my parents never did it at all! Did yours? I don't think so.

Nell is ten years older and Gracey is ten years younger. We were, each of us, like "only children." Dad said he raised his own baby-sitters. I was getting ready to go to my Christmastime piano recital—I was playing *Humoresque*—when I sat down at home to have one last rehearsal and Mom came through the living room in an odd frock. My mother was always beautifully dressed; she had true innate style, never flashy, just plain chic. But this dress she had on for the Christmastime recital— yuck! It was a dark green crepe that fell loose from a yoke at her shoulders and had a thin red ribbon tied loosely around her middle, not the way Mom usually dressed. I whispered to Nell who was twenty, "Yuck—Mom looks like she's gonna have a baby in that dress."

Nell, leaping at an opportunity, said loudly, "What did you say? Momma, did you hear what Bubba said?"

"Shhhhhhh," I whispered, mortified.

"What did you say, honey?" asked Mom, all smiles.

Timidly I answered, "It looks like you're gonna have a baby in that dress."

"Well, what would you say if I told you I was?"

I burst into tears, my head down on the keyboard, just weeping. She sat down on the bench beside me and put her arm around my waist.

"Honey?" she said, puzzled.

"Could it be a baby sister, Mom, could it be a baby sister?"

A few months later, in the middle of the night when Dad called from the hospital, I didn't believe him. I thought he was kiddin' me. But he wasn't. On May 17, 1949, Gracey came into my life, and she's just the best girl in the whole world. I love my little sister so much. I got her to walk really early so I could teach her to dance. I had it in my head we would be the next Fred and Adele Astaire, but like most parents who push their kids into doing what *they* do, I pushed Gracey too hard and fast and she went off horseback riding. It wasn't till I left for college that she discovered dancing for herself, and today she's a terrific tap dancer and teacher and does enormous and respected work in elevating this subjugated American art form.

I was named for my two nonexistent grandfathers,

*With my sister, Gracey, at
four and fourteen.

*With Gracey, years later,
looking like the Carpenters.

Thomas and James. My sister was named for our two grandmothers, the bitch and the witch, Grace and Adella. Nell never liked *her* name very much, and when we took to calling the new baby Dell, I heard Nell remark under her breath, "Nell, Dell and Hell, they all rhyme." I think that's when I started calling our new sister "Bitsy." Nell was already "Gussie," and I was "Bubba." Gussie, Bitsy, and Bubba, what a trio. Two, twelve, twenty-two—always ten years apart. Strange, ain't it?

I think I was present at Gracey's conception. I remember it was a hot summer, and I was supposed to be next door at Mama Dow's house listening to soap operas on the radio in her upstairs sewing room—*Lorenzo Jones and His Wife Belle, Backstage Wife, The Story of Larry and Mary Noble* ("Can a simple girl from the country find happiness married to Broadway's brightest star?"), and my favorite, *Ma Perkins*. I loved radio. It took you on flights of fancy from which television only robs you. Quincy Jones remembers that "radio was a powerful escape into the imagination," and he's right. We listened to *The Green Hornet, Inner Sanctum, The Bell Telephone Hour,* and all the "preacher" shows Grandma Tune loved. These radio broadcasts were *the* home entertainment of my childhood. Add the occasional grown-up movie Mom would take me to because I was a perfect child and the Saturday Morning Fun Club at our local movie house, and that was the cultural diet of the times. No wonder I was always putting on shows in the backyard! Anyway, this one particular warm afternoon, not a breeze stirring in Mama Dow's sewing room, I was rest-

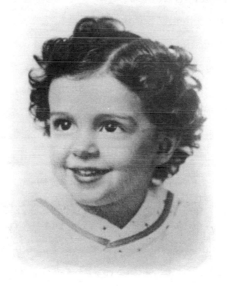

*With Twiggy backstage after I won the
most beautiful baby contest. The cast
thought this picture was of Nana Visitor,
Twiggy's understudy. Twiggy thought I
looked more like Judy Garland.

less and not the least bit interested in Ma Perkins's latest dilemmas, so I came home early. Now, back then, there was never a locked door in our house or in the whole neighborhood, in fact. Life was so innocent and trustworthy and honest. In through the screen door I came, not slamming it—I'd been broken of that habit quickly—through the living room, down the hall toward my bedroom, and there's the bathroom door, closed—I tested it—locked. The bathroom door was *locked*—I didn't even know you *could* lock it. I knocked—something was wrong. "What's going on?" says I.

"Bubba?" says Dad in an odd voice.

"Go on back to Mama Dow's, Honey," says Mom in a tone I'd never heard before.

"What's wrong?" I ask.

"Go on back to Mama Dow's."

I felt my chest tighten. I couldn't breathe. I stumbled out into the front yard and knelt under our giant acorn tree and cried and cried. As I write this, I don't know what I was thinking—in fact, I wasn't thinking—I was just feeling something, and nine months later Gracey was born. Children know things, things we've forgotten.

I wonder if the reason I've never really grown up—except physically—is because I learned to dance too soon, or because I was old before my time, so I've spent my life "youthening." I do remember going to Sheila Jones's third birthday party and Mom asking how it was. Four-year-old doubting Tommy answered skeptically, "Her said her was three, but her don't look three to me." Was

*Doubting Tommy,
looking very Prada.

little Sheila Jones trying to pull a fast one on me, lying about her age? What *was* I thinking in my four-year-old brain? What am I thinking in my fifty-seven-year-old brain? I have always lacked emotional maturity. "Oh, Tune, you're just an overgrown kid!" I've heard the likes of that on many occasions and taken it as a compliment. But is it? As I write this, this early Manhattan morning in Penthouse C, I find myself struggling through yet another doomed relationship. Why do I keep trying? It's all so seemingly futile. Grow up!

✶The news was out on the "Broadway Gypsy grapevine" that Jule Styne was producing the big show for the opening of Caesar's Palace in Las Vegas. We're in the sixties now. Rumor had it that Caesar's Palace was to be the most lavish hotel casino ever built and that the showroom was beyond belief. Auditions for boy dancers were held in Variety Arts, West 46th Street, between Broadway and 8th Avenue at 10:00 A.M. I was there. There was another guy exactly my height named Eddie James—we even looked alike (he later married Juliet Prowse). The choreographer liked our twinship and the way we danced. Eliminations were made; we, among others, were kept and told to return at 1:00 P.M. to sing for Jule Styne. Yikes.

I always get so nervous at auditions, with that terrible feeling of having to prove you have talent instead of merely sharing it by entertaining the folks. I used to think of the people out front at an audition as the enemy. Now that I'm out front a lot at auditions I have a completely different take on it. Auditionees, listen up! We out front want you to be brilliant. The sooner we get our talented cast, the sooner the highly imperfect system called auditioning is finished and we can start rehearsals. The people out front are not the enemy, they are your biggest fans. "Please let them dazzle us," we're saying. "Let them be perfect." If you believe this, perhaps that could lessen the pressures of auditioning, pressures which make one put up walls of protection around one's own natural personality and gift. This pressure sometimes causes a distancing effect and sometimes creates a pushed frantic quality that's not one's natural bent, but sort of a manufactured gaiety to overcompensate for the discomfort and, yes, *fear.* Just know we're on your side. As a director, I do my best to create a nourishing atmosphere for the "fragile plants to grow." I think other directors do likewise. Trust us, and do your best. Shine through.

Back to the Caesar's Palace audition. We had an hour to kill, and both Eddie and I were nervous about singing for Jule Styne. We went to the Rum House in the Hotel Edison and had a drink. I can't believe I did it. I've never gone on stage to perform except au naturel, but this one audition was the exception. And what an exception! The rum and Coke must have relaxed me. I was ushered into the hall, introduced to Jule Styne, sang my eight bars of "You Gotta Have Heart," finished, headed for the door, and he yelled, "Stop! Sing some more."

I didn't have any more music. I thought of my favorite song. I asked the pianist, "Do you know 'Time After Time'?"

He didn't.

Jule said, "I know it; I'll play it for you."

I sang it and sang it well. He played it great. He loved my rendition, and I loved his. I complimented him, "Hey, that was great."

"Thanks," he quipped. "It ought to be; I wrote it!"

I honestly didn't know that Jule Styne had composed "Time After Time," but I definitely scored some points with my choice.

"Meet me in my office in the Mark Hellinger Theatre tomorrow at two o'clock and bring every song you know." What a shock! Is this how it works? When I arrived the next day Jule had assembled Betty Comden, Adolph Green, Phyllis Newman, the great vocal arranger Buster Davis, and a couple of more notables I can't remember. He hit the keyboard, and I sang for an hour. We CLICKED.

"I'm gonna send you to my tailor, kid, I'm gonna groom ya', put together an act for ya', and season ya' in the Catskills as Jule Styne's New Singing Discovery. You'll do 'All I Need Is the Girl' and pick out a gal from the audience and bring her up onstage and dance with her. Buster, I want you to start coaching him every day. Meet me at my apartment next Monday and show me what you've accomplished."

Wow! What a break! My big break! It's just like in the movies.

Next day, Buster was a master. He did an arrangement of "Old Devil Moon" that was really exciting. We put together a few more songs in the next three days. Jule was set to conduct the overture for *Gypsy* at Lincoln Center on Sunday, and then, come Monday, I'd be doing my "new act" for him.

I arrived at his penthouse a little early. I was greeted at the door of his all-green domicile by his beautiful red-headed wife Margaret. She was quite pale. Hadn't I heard? While conducting the symphony orchestra last night he had collapsed on the podium. He would be all right but must have a complete rest. And he did. He went on to write more musicals. And Caesar's Palace opened. And I never heard from him again until I became successful on my own. It was like the whole thing had never happened. But it had.

It's always surprising in life how one thing leads to another. Piecing together the patches of my living quilt I realize that at the time the incidents are occurring it all seems so normal, so accidental. However, taking a look from the present, the past seems without accident, like there's some grand design to one's living quilt that's beyond one's control or even comprehension. Here's a specific example of what I mean.

On the elevator up to the Jule Styne Caesar's Palace audition, this dynamic little guy stepped on, looked up at me and said, "Well, hello, who are you?"

I've always been embarrassed about my name. It

sounds so made up, so corny, so cute, so young, so happy, so phony, so *short*, but *it's my real name.* When I was under contract to 20th Century–Fox, Gene Kelly suggested to me that I change it to something "more realistic." He felt it would be limiting, and he was right. I've always had a huge desire to play *Dracula* onstage. After Frank Langella had his big success with it on Broadway, he was replaced by Raul Julia, and after Raul came Jean Le Clerque. Then it was time to tour the show, and I canvassed for the role. Eric Schepard, my agent, woke me up to the truth. "Lookit," he said, "Tommy Tune in *Dracula*? Sounds like a joke." He was right. Jose Greco got the part. At least it went to a dancer! The count *should* move across the stage with the stealth of a trained dancer, but he shouldn't be named Tommy Tune. At Fox we played the Name Tommy Tune Game. Everybody I met on the lot I consulted. "Look at me. What would *you* call me?" Irene Sharaff suggested "Tom Cabot." I thought, "Why not Tom Lodge?" Roger Edens joked, "Ben Dover." Somebody else, "Clay Rawlins." I listened. I tried. Ixnay!

So here's this guy many years earlier on the elevator at Variety Arts saying "Well, hello, who are you?"

I said, "My name is Tommy Tune. Do you think I should change it?"

He answered, "Not if you want to go around being Tommy Tune."

"Good advice," I thought. Who *else* would I want to go around being? "And what's your name?" I ventured.

"Michael Bennett."

*Name that Tune.
Two shots from the Hollywood years.

He told me he had just received his first choreographic assignment for a show headed for Broadway. It was called *A Joyful Noise* and was to star John Raitt. He was Bonnie's dad even then before the world knew her. Michael explained he was going up to a studio to pre-produce some dance vocabulary for the show.

"After your Caesar's Palace audition stop in and see what we're doing!"

So after the audition I did. What work he had created! Sixteen counts of absolutely original choreography that my body still knows all these years later. I dropped my dance bag and learned it on the spot. I had to. It was great. That was my introduction to Michael Bennett. Eventually I turned down the Caesar's Palace job and signed on to dance for Michael in his Broadway debut. His choreography drew raves, and *A Joyful Noise* closed in two weeks. Sad but not so bad. That meeting on the elevator changed the course of my entire life. I formed a personal and professional alliance with Michael Bennett that lasted for many years. What an important patch in my living quilt!

✶ It's the late seventies, I'm a director now, and it's the first day of rehearsal for *Cloud 9*, a play by Caryl Churchill, which was absolutely riddled with original thought. What a thinker and brave woman she is! I'd spent the night, tossing and turning, longing for sleep and asking for some kind of divine guidance to get me through the first day of rehearsal. I've always felt the director earns his full keep by knowing what to say or do on that first empty morning of rehearsal for a new play. How does he get the ball rolling? Actors gathered, contracts signed, coffee and Danish served, Equity meeting held, Equity meeting finished, producers and staff introduced, break—Mr. Director, you're on. Get the ball rolling. It's your job. This was my first nonmusical assignment as a director in New York, and I was feeling the pressure of perhaps being considered not much more than a glorified choreographer. *Cloud 9* was dealing with some dangerous themes for those times, and the climate in America was, well, less than open, especially if compared to that of sophisticated Olde England.

Judging by the relatively cool audience reactions at the Royal Court, the London production of *Cloud 9* seemed almost a trifle. True, budget limitations there had prevented much of a physical mounting, but sometimes that's a blessing, allowing the theatergoer to concentrate on the words and not the works. It was very well acted, but something was missing for me—I needed to plunge deeper into what Caryl had written.

But how? Here I am in the tiny hours of the morning—it's still dark, and I'm rolling around, asking for the "know how."

It came. Laurence Olivier appeared at the foot of my bed—this is not a dream, I'm awake—much more than an apparition. He was smiling and "tsk-tsking," one hand to the side of his face.

"Well," says I. "What do I do?"

He said, "My dear boy, it's all of it, *all* of it, simply an expression of love." Those were his exact words.

I went to rehearsal at 10:00 A.M., and here's what I said:

> There is this feeling, desire, need, longing within each of us, to *share* ourselves with another human being on this earth. They can be of the same sex, different sex, older, younger, same color, different color—doesn't matter. We all want to share ourselves and unless we cut out our human hearts there is no way of stopping this feeling, this desire, this need, this longing. That is what *Cloud 9* addresses. Last night, Sir Laurence Olivier appeared at the foot of my bed and said, "My dear boy, it's all of it, *all* of it, simply an expression of love."

We went to work. Years later at the Broadway opening night party of *My One and Only* at the Tavern on the Green, with my costar Twiggy, I sat at a round table with Maggie Smith, Lauren Bacall, Joan Plowright, and Sir Laurence himself. I told him of this prerehearsal episode in which he'd appeared, and, astonished, he said, "But my dear boy, that's what I always say to my casts on first day—'It's simply an expression of love.'"

*Cloud 9* was a big success, and people still talk about

*Opening night at the Tavern
on the Green, with Twiggy
and the Oliviers.

it today in reverential tones. Mike Nichols, on opening night said one word to me, "Perfect!" Lee Grant could not get out of her seat afterward. Phil Oesterman wouldn't leave the theater. Bea Arthur kept asking me questions about how we arrived at this and that. Shirley MacLaine held her breath. The production was praised, and I owe it all to Sir Laurence and, of course, wonderful Caryl Churchill.

What is this need to share ourselves—whether the world wants us or not—is it ego? Is it creativity? What is this thing called love? I'm not sure, but I do know it's necessary, if life is to continue on this planet. Yet every year it seems more unattainable as the scar tissue builds up around my heart. Each year the candle burns dimmer, but it is still alight. I wonder if I'll ever find a match, someone to hold me and tell me it's gonna be all right, someone to share my life with, the other half of me, someone with whom I'm whole, someone who can take it—I'm a handful, a full plate, no leftovers. Good luck.

It remains an irony for me that in the midst of what appears a success I find my "lonely place" aching. I'm standing on a big stage, and the audience is on its feet, applauding, smiling, cheering; the lights are bright, the music plays, I take a final bow, I wave, and the curtain falls. Two hours later I drop the keys to my hotel room door on the coffee table, and there is only silence. No one to ask, "How'd it go, Honey?" like Mom always said to Dad. So what do you do after the show? After the theater empties?

Well, if I define myself only in terms of success, it makes the lonely place more chilling. But if I can spread my interest into the world, reroute my single track into a multitrack organism, and head myself into the direction of inquisitiveness, knowing that I don't know anything, claiming the blank canvas instead of fleeing from it, I find solace. Praying really works, too, on your knees, praying for others and asking God for help. If I can just deflect all the sympathy for me into a keen empathic interest in the people of the world, in the very act of giving to the world instead of demanding that the world give to me, suddenly a miracle occurs, and the lonely place recedes.

And what is a miracle? Marianne Williamson says that a miracle is a change in perception. By changing your perception of a situation you can get through it, but for how long? Until the next time the key hits the table in an empty hotel room.

Living is a constant process; there is no trick to it, just simply taking each moment at its fullest. There is no past, there is no future, there is only now. And right now, I'm sitting, writing, breathing; a plane is going over, the sun is shining, my dog Ophie is flopped out next to me on the sofa breathing easily, and my fingers are clutching this pen with a purpose. I'm fervently seeking to communicate with you. Right now you're holding this book, reading these words, breathing, too, just like me, and light is falling on the printed page. It's like that; you add up all these observations as they occur, and it's a life. It's all we have. It's all so completely simplistic, so frustratingly complex. Will I ever learn my lines? Will I ever remember them? This is not a dress rehearsal. This is the show.

In the fifties Martha Graham came to speak at the University of Texas. It was in a medium-sized auditorium, it was packed, and she was a pure illumination. After her talk she opened the floor to questions. One Texas-accented girl in the back asked, "Miz Graham, you said 'all great dancin' stems from the lonely place.' Where *is* the lonely place, Miz Graham?" Without pause she entoned, "Between your thighs. Next question." Gasps all around. This was the fifties you know! "The lonely place." I should be a much better dancer than I am.

✶ "I've written a book about Martha but I have to wait for her to die to release it!" announced Agnes de Mille. It was a great afternoon. It was in her apartment downtown. We had lunch in her dining room. She had white enameled wrought iron garden furniture—glass table top and curlicue chairs with little cushions—I really didn't fit into them at all, but I'm used to that. Airplanes, taxis, cramped theater seats—I've learned to adapt. I'm a collapsible dancer. The silverware and china were totally mismatched, and there was a lone paper napkin stuck in a water glass. Her Jamaican housekeeper had done her best.

This was after Agnes's stroke, so she was physically

compromised. She sighed and said wistfully, "I used to set such a nice table."

We ate, she talked, I asked as many questions as I could.

"Twenty years without a complimentary review from the *New York Times* has almost killed me." She spoke of her early struggles and her early successes—the woman who changed the form of the American musical forever. There's *Oklahoma!* (Agnes de Mille), *West Side Story* (Jerome Robbins), and *A Chorus Line* (Michael Bennett). Notice the order—I'm with the pioneer. Coming from the East, I wondered how she was able to capture the great expanse of the West in her choreography.

"Well, you must remember, my husband was a Texan." Then adding with a kittenish lopsided grin, "and almost as tall as you."

We spoke of painting and music. I told her the story of when I was a chorus boy on Broadway making ninety dollars a week. I would pass by this gallery in my neighborhood, and I had fallen for this painting in the window. Realistically depicted in oil was a near broken-down wooden ship, sails ripped and blowing in the wind against a blue sky, sitting—kerplunk—in a field of golden wheat. What an image—this great ship plowing ahead and not advancing one iota. Finally I got the nerve to go in and price it, suspecting that any art was out of my range. The owner said, "Sorry, it's sold. Agnes de Mille bought it. She said it reminded her of herself."

Agnes said, "Oh, yes, I remember that painting—it

was done by one of my ex-dancers, Margaret Taylor—
you'd like each other. I'll make another lunch so you
can meet."

Later in the afternoon she remembered that after her
stroke, as her husband was lifting her into her bed, she
had whispered, "I apologize for ruining your life." He
had responded, "Nonsense, Aggie, you've made me a
better man."

She was back in her bed now, using a pink, faded terrycloth towel to blot the spittle from the corner of her
mouth that drooped since the stroke. "It's time for you
to go now."

"But wait," I thought, "I've got so much more to ask
you." Panicked that this might be my one and only
chance, I begged for one more question: "You're such a
good writer. How do you do that? How do you write?"

"Ah, well, now, that's *hard*," she said sternly. And that
was it! She's right. She pulled out a small photograph of
herself as a young woman and signed it to me, and I
was out—out on the sidewalk as the sun was setting.
Here was the park she'd walked the perimeter of for a
whole day and night while she conceived *Rodeo*. I
walked the perimeter, right then and there—I had to—
following in Aggie's footsteps.

A couple of weeks later I got a note from her inviting
me to tea to meet the artist, "And you can bring that girl
you kept on talking about (during lunch I had spoken
about my current dancing partner, Annie Reinking) if
you want." I couldn't, I had to go on tour with Annie in
*Bye Bye Birdie*. I never saw Agnes de Mille again.

*Sometime in the eighties I had another interesting lunch. It was with Ruth Gordon and Garson Kanin at the Russian Tea Room. I'd watched and admired her from afar for many years and, of course, Garson Kanin is quite a guy and such a perfect gentleman with her. He loved her so very much.

Once, in a coast-to-coast plane crossing, she held my eyeballs riveted. I couldn't look away, everything she did was so interesting. What she drank looked like scotch. What she wore was a scarf tied over her head, pirate style, with what looked like a black captain's hat on top, the bill at a jaunty angle, a miniskirt, and white go-go boots. Now that was personal style, and it worked on Ruth Gordon. I'd known about Ruth Gordon since I attended Lamar High School in Houston. We did an autobiographical play she wrote called *Years Ago*, a sort of family drama that was extremely funny, laced with tender, moving moments: Young girl from Boston sees matinee performance of the great actress Hazel Dawn at the Colonial Theatre and is smitten with the idea of going into show business. Her father is a tyrannical sea captain, and her mother reads *Unity*. It was all true and had a very specific ring to it that the truth always has, thus making it universal.

After the plane landed, waiting at the baggage claim, I continued to observe her every move. She's the only person who's ever gotten away with using Louis Vuitton luggage; hers was vintage with her initials embossed in tarnished gold—R.G.J. (Ruth Gordon Jones)—and this luggage had *toured*. It was beat up and scarred and scuffed and absolutely beautiful. In clothing, accoutrements, and people, I've always preferred the bruised peach. Beautiful women and men after their blooming season, just as perfection starts to turn—what an exquisite time of life—so vulnerable, and they don't know it yet, or if they do, they don't know how to live with it, the loss of prime. Exquisite. It's so much more compelling than perfection.

Lunchtime with Ruth and Garson at the Russian Tea Room was a show that day. David Merrick at one table, Shirley MacLaine and Kenneth Tynan's widow at another, Kitty Carlisle Hart and an unknown society doyenne, Sam Cohn and one of his top talents, I can't remember who, but I really remember Ruth Gordon that day.

She had great stories. One about Thornton Wilder, my favorite playwright, and her going to a brothel together. "We wanted to see a woman and a dog. The madam who had just promised she'd show us anything we wanted was shocked at our request and sent us on our way with a remarkable gesture." She demonstrated. I can't describe it here, but if you ask me, I'll show you. It's emblazoned on my memory.

She talked about how she stopped smoking. Here's how: She only smoked in the bathroom, and when the urge came she removed herself from all the fun to sit alone on the john and puff away. But then she'd hear all the laughter outside that she was missing and couldn't bear it. "Ruth," she'd say to herself, "it's cigarettes or fun." And guess which won! Now this was way before all this smoking ban stuff; it was something Ruth Gordon had invented for herself to get over the addiction, and I thought it was damned clever.

She told me about Fred Astaire. He was in a Broadway musical called *The Gay Divorce* by Cole Porter and did an impossible dance number to "Night and Day." "How do you do it, Freddy," she asked him. "How do you do it?" "Well, Ruth," Fred said, "I come into the theater every day at five, and I do the entire dance by myself on the empty stage in the empty theater. Then at night while I'm getting through it in front of the audience I say to myself, 'Fred, you did it once, you can do it again.'" This works. Oh yes, this really works; I've tried it.

I suppose that's why Ruth Gordon went over the entire script of whatever play she was appearing in at 5:00 P.M. before each and every performance. At night, I wonder if she said to herself, "Ruth, you did it once, you can do it again."

She wore very orange makeup—it looked like old-fashioned grease paint, and I wouldn't be surprised if it was, seems fittin'—and her cute legs were bound in narrow strips of Ace bandages, wrapped all the way up and disappearing underneath her miniskirt. She held me and Garson, too, enthralled. He's heard every story a hundred times I'm sure, but she was so fascinatin' that she could have been reading us recipes and we would have taken them for Shakespeare. In truth she *was* giving us recipes. Recipes for life, her menu on getting through it. The hours went by like minutes, and the lunch crowd emptied out of the Russian Tea Room. As we reentered the bright, sunny, crisp day in New York City she said,

"Hey, this was great. We gotta do this again, we're just gettin' started." Garson and I were heading to his office in Carnegie Hall to talk business, and I watched Ruth Gordon disappear into the crowd at 6th Avenue and 57th Street. "We gotta do this again, we're just gettin' started." That was the last time I saw her.

*The one and only time I saw Fred Astaire was backstage after a performance at the Music Center in Los Angeles. For our West Coast engagement of *My One and Only* seemingly every movie star in Hollywood came out. It was so exciting, every night of our run. Most theater people never want to know who's out front. I *always* want to know. It helps me be specific. Tonight it's Esther Williams. "Oh, she's gonna love the water dance—I'll think of her out there as I'm splashing around in the tank." Rudy Vallee? "I'd better *croon* tonight. Or croon *better*." It's all part of my theory for keeping the performance fresh. Know somebody out front and do it *specifically* for them. It avoids the general and slightly colors that night's presentation with a fresh hue. "Long-run-itis" is a virus that can deaden a show. I liken a long-run production to a beautiful flower arrangement that's dried out. Everything's still in place but the moisture is gone. Beware! So, I love to know who's out front. It

\*Tommy and Minnie and Twiggy
and Mickey, the Disney version of
*Bob and Carol and Ted and Alice.*

could be a cast member's mom, a politician, my dentist, anyone *specific*. However, I did tell the stage manager if Fred Astaire should come, "Don't tell me." I'd be afraid to *walk* in front of my idol, much less *dance*.

*My One and Only* was a musical with a Gershwin score formed predominantly of tunes from *Funny Face*, a musical that Fred had done originally with his sister Adele on Broadway and later in the movies with Audrey Hepburn. Now, it was Twiggy and me, and let's face it, we were no Fred and Adele or even Fred and Audrey. We were Twiggy and Tommy Tune, and we entertained a lot of audiences. We were unique but I don't think you'd call us classic. If this sounds modest, at least it's not false, and I don't mean to belittle the show. However, we were simply a flop in our out-of-town tryout in Boston until Mike Nichols came in and totally saved us. I suppose Mike Nichols is truly the best man. Certainly he's the best man *I* know. A more brilliant mind, a bigger heart, and a funnier sense of humor you'll not find. He's my favorite man on the planet, and I treasure every moment I've ever spent with him. Unbilled and hugely generous with his time, care, and talent, he completely overhauled *My One and Only*, and any success that it enjoyed—and it was a big hit—was directly attributable to Mike Nichols, my hero. During our run we'd been visited backstage by a galaxy—Charlton Heston, Kirk Douglas, Julie Andrews, Gene Kelly, Joan Rivers, Cher, Tony Bennett, Carol Burnett, Liza Minnelli, Quincy Jones, Angie Dickinson, Miles

*Holding Twiggy, *My One and Only*,
St. James Theatre, New York.

*My One and Only* team, Phillip Oesterman,
Peter Stone, T 'n' T, Mike Nichols.
We had fun. We made a hit.

Davis, Donald Sutherland, Dustin Hoffman, Jacqueline Bisset, Lucille Ball, Warren Beatty, Sammy Davis Jr., and on and on—"but don't tell me if Fred comes."

On this particular night onstage, warming up before the show with the house curtain in, for some unknown reason I was compelled to peer out of the peephole—I never do this—and holy shit, there he sits, perfectly centered in the peephole. Intake of air, breathing stops, a cold sweat pops out of every pore, and I completely forget every piece of choreography in the show. Do I start on my left or my right? What do I do with my hands? Why are they growing bigger? The tempo is too slow, the tempo is too fast. It was the worst of times, it was the best of times. What a night! I remember nothing. The songs sang themselves, someone else apparently spoke my lines, and my feet never connected with the floor. Afterward, we met, and the first words out of my idol's mouth were, "You're a *tall* son of a bitch!" Then he laughed so hard at himself like he couldn't believe he'd said it. He loved the show and kept asking me how I did it.

"How can you do that every night?"

"What do you mean?"

"I mean how can you do that every night?"

I answered, "I go over it every day, and when I'm out there every night I keep saying to myself, "Tommy, you did it once, you can do it again." I could detect that it rang a distant bell, and his eyes twinkled. What a gent. What a star. What a dancing man! I adore Fred Astaire.

The next day this note arrived:

Sept. 10

Dear Tommy—

I feel compelled to again tell you how much I enjoyed *My One and Only*! And your excellent work! It is a show of many highlights and wonderful surprises. It's easy for me to see why you have such a big hit with it. The cast was indeed excellent! Wow!

Best wishes always—<br>Fred A—

Even his handwriting dances. They don't make 'em like that anymore.

&#42; I'm always getting in on the tail end of things, or at least I feel things are always ending and I'm left watching. I'd been with my very first boyfriend for about a year down in Texas. One night at dinner with a group of friends all laughing and eating and drinking, he quite casually mentioned that he'd decided to go to New York. And he did. Just like that. I stayed and finished college, and I never saw him again. Years later I heard through the grapevine that he had been killed. Life can be really casual sometimes, leaving a person with a feeling of no gravity. My primary tap dancing teacher in Texas, Camille Long Hill, told me once, "Tommy, you've got

\*Camille Long Hill, my tap teacher.
I have been so blessed with great
guides. Camille was a sage.

your head in the clouds, be sure to keep your feet on the ground." Good advice. She called me once to tell me she was sending me something, to watch out for it. Then Mom called to tell me that Camille had died in her sleep. Two days later a parcel post package arrived. It was a full-length velvety purple theater robe she'd made for me. I still wear it, and I think, "Tommy, you've got your head in the clouds, be sure to keep your feet on the ground."

But sometimes this lack of gravitational pull frightens me. I feel like I just might rise off the surface of the earth and just keep going. Is this what they mean by "light in the loafers"? Do *real* people feel this way, too? I was told by a psychic reader once that I am an alien, that I am not from this planet and that I did the best I could in adapting my physicality into something that could pass but that it hasn't quite worked.

"What?" says I.

"Well, look at you," she said, "Your hands, legs, your torso, neck, and head, they're not like people from this earth, but you've done the best job you could in trying to create a normal body. You're a *seer* from another planet, Tommy, and you were sent down here to do this work— on the way down they hadn't decided if you should be a man or a woman, but just before entry you gotta load of how it worked down here and made a quick decision."

Should I believe this? Down deep somewhere it has a ring of truth. I'd always wondered why I'm a size small but stretched to an extra extra long. I've never been able

*"A dude from a different planet."
Well, just *look* at me. I've
done my best to fit in.

to buy clothes off the rack if I want them to fit. My waist is thirty-one inches and tall shops start at thirty-four inches. My inseam and arm lengths are off the chart when measured up to my waist and collar size. I'm six foot six and a half and weigh 160 pounds. This is not normal, but then as the character in *The Fantasticks* prays, "Please, God, please don't let me be normal." No problem there.

Andy Warhol and I used to do "cum" facials, using our own, of course, not each others. He'd heard Mae West used to do it, too. Of course, she couldn't use her own. She used what the musclemen in her club act produced for her. I wonder if it works better if it's somebody else's?

If I *did* come from another planet, it certainly would account for a lot of my puzzlement with earthlings. I mean how come men get to go around without their shirts on and women don't? I've always been a big fan of breasts, maybe because I was bottle fed. Maybe I feel cheated, and that accounts for my obsession with tits. At some point my taste broadened to include pecs, too, but not too many men like their pecs romanced, or at least I haven't found many. There have been some notable exceptions though, and the hours I've spent "breast feeding" in my adulthood on both sexes have been quite pleasurable. On men they're called "dunes"; on women they're called "pillows." Either way they make people from my planet go, "Yum-yum," and send us into ecstasy. I don't pretend to understand this semifetish, and it would take years of analysis, which I haven't undergone, to clarify this weirdness, but maybe, anatomically, because the breast area houses the heart, I am simply and instinctually going for the center of love. We all want love. Let it be. Maybe I'll outgrow it.

Then there's the controversial issue of peeing in the shower, which I really enjoy—water to water. And, of course, my favorite state—laughing and crying at the exact same time—to be so happy and sad that you are laughing out loud and crying at the sadness of it all simultaneously. That's a magic state, and it doesn't happen often. It's sort of like one of those magic performances when the experience and the experienced *combine* in time and space, and you are no longer doing the moves or singing the songs or saying the lines but it is all happening because it *has* to—it's inevitable and it is being sent to you from somewhere else—is it that particular "combine" of entities in the audience? Like the Fred Astaire night? Maybe. Is it from on high? Probably, but it's not something you can summon up for yourself. All you can do is ask for it—and I do—before and during every performance, and sometimes, if I'm living right, it happens and it's a miracle. It's the reason I can keep going—maybe it will happen again. Like love— maybe, if I'm living right—I'll get to fall in love again. You have to ask for it and then just give it up, and sometimes it happens.

＊In kindergarten my most vivid memory is the May fete held each year on the first of the month. The finale of the big outdoor event, which took place on the huge green lawn surrounding my elementary school, was the ritualistic winding of the May Pole by the sixth-grade girls. The alternating pink and white ribbons were pulled out tight from the top of the pole. The girls with the pink ribbons circled clockwise, the white, counter-clockwise—up and over and under and beneath, round and round—until the pole was braided. Then dropping the ends of the ribbons, the sixth-grade girls made elaborate curtsies to the pole, and the ceremony was complete. What did it mean? I wonder if it was some form of phallus worship.

The May fete began with the entrance of the teachers to "Pomp and Circumstance," then each grade, beginning with kindergarten, performed their piece. Our piece was a partner dance performed in long double lines across the lawn. Each little boy held both hands of his pretty little girl partner—heel-toe, heel-toe. There was just one problem: There weren't enough little girls to go around so I had a boy for a partner. Hmmm. His name was Boydie Austen, and he was a terrible dancer. He did "side-side" when he was supposed to do "front-back." I asked the teacher, Miss Miia (she pronounced it My-Ay), why I had to have Boydie for a partner. I was "put out" with the arrangement. She explained that she had to put the *good* dancers with the ones who were having trouble so that the routine would go smoothly. I

\*In kindergarten. I'm top row, second from right,
and none too happy. Perhaps the reason is
top row, second from left, the infamous
Boydie Austen. Yuk!

liked the flattery and did my best to haul Boydie Austen around.

Was I my brother's keeper? No, I was his dancing partner.

The May fetes were great shows, and I looked forward to them every spring. Then one year over the P.A. system it was announced that there would be no more May Day festivities: something about Communism. I didn't get it, but that was the end of the May fete. It was such a beautiful tradition and made everyone feel so good. I've missed them ever since, but not Boydie Austen.

\*I wouldn't want to suggest, with the somewhat frivolous tone of these memories, that I haven't had hardships and turmoil, and that I haven't risen to certain difficult occasions with the courage a man needs. I've taken care of a lot of business, and as lucky as I gratefully am, I've endured some unseemly struggles and somehow prevailed. Of course there's always a bigger mission at stake, the work itself, and with the help and trust of the people who surround me and guidance from above, the larger picture has reached completion. One of my most severe struggles and eventually a source of pride was *Grand Hotel: The Musical.*

Jack Lee, the seasoned Broadway musical director,

brought me a script by Luther Davis. As linear as it was, which didn't interest me, there was a phrase that caught my imagination, and suddenly a vision of how to bring this old chestnut to the stage began growing upon that beautiful empty stage in my head. I once did a self-portrait: shoulders, neck; and sitting on top, steadily balanced, was a large vacant stage where my head should be—curtains open, brick back wall with floor boards radiating out, the ever present "ghost light" (a standard with an electrical cable running off into the wings), and a bright incandescent bulb shining out into the empty space. That's what I am when I'm at my best—a body with an empty stage for a head, waiting, waiting to be filled with the latest bit of make-believe.

The composers of *Grand Hotel* were Bob Wright and Chet Forrest, old pals of musical director Jack Lee, and after reading the script I went along with Jack to hear the score. I always read the script first because I am so easily seduced by music. But if there is no story, there is no musical, no matter how great the score. I have learned this the hard way  by experience. An earlier project, *Nine*, was my professor, and through those classes I've become a better student. *Nine* was a big success but I was always aware of the smoke and mirrors that I'd created to divert the viewer from the fact that it lacked a plot. *Nine* was based on Fellini's film *8½*, which had no plot either, but in a movie that's not terribly important, especially if you're Fellini, a master visionary. Onstage, however, making lyric theater, a powerhouse plot is very important. Movies are dreams; theater pieces need to portray life-altering situations. I didn't know this when I assumed the directing/choreographing reins on *Nine*. A tape of Maury Yeston's score had been slipped through the letter box opening of my apartment's front door and found its way onto my sound system. I loved it immediately and committed myself to the project. Whoops, no plot. Mario Fratti's libretto was interesting, but more like a play than a musical and too conventional to accommodate Maury's dreamy music. The gifted playwright Arthur Kopit hopped on board and added his particular brand of surrealism to the mix. Welcome. I had only one collision with the authors during the making of *Nine*, but it was a doozy.

Our working script was in place, and we began the auditioning process. The cast breakdown was of the conventional sort. The leading character, Guido, was to be played by Raul Julia, and he was perfect. I canvassed for Karen Akers, the cabaret and recording artist, to make her stage debut as his wife. I remember Arthur wanting more of an "actress" and Maury wanting more "vocal range," but when she auditioned we all knew that she was *it*. She was nominated for a Tony for her portrayal. Anita Morris was cast in the blink of an eye as Guido's mistress and was astounding in the role and also nominated for a Tony. Taina Elg, the splendid Finnish actress was to play the mother, but when it came time to cast the German producer who in the

*I endeavored to inject Raul Julia, who played Guido
(Fellini), with the "director spirit" and asked him to
rehearse his role for *Nine the Musical* beside me out
front. Raul was such a vital man. Our planet is much
diminished without him, and much diminished
without Fellini, too. I've worn black since the maestro
died and I'm finding it hard to break the habit.
Too much black can turn in on one.

script was called Otto we had our contretemps. I simply found no interesting men in New York City for the role. Most character actors of a certain age these days seem to have deserted Broadway for television land out West. And why not? There's plenty of work in Los Angeles for mature actors who usually have families to support, and we all know how much easier life is in California than in New York. So I have seen our bank of experienced mature actors depleted through my years of workin' Broadway.

Out of nowhere arrives this glamorous French ex-ballerina /ex-Folies-Bergère star dressed head to toe in bright red. What an entrance! Liliane Montevecchi. She *had* to be in the show, but what part? There was no part. And yet . . . I sat up in the middle of the night and knew. She would play Otto—just change the sex and the country—from male to female, from Germany to France. And while we're at it, why not cast the entire show—save Raul and his younger self, Guido at age nine—with women? Make it a celebration of women. Let's put the entire show into the imagination of Guido, who was actually a stand-in for Fellini himself. How would he create his world? Being the woman-lover/womanizer he was, the answer seemed natural. All women. Every role.

Well, my collaborators thought I'd lost it. Arthur thought I meant to have females performing male roles in drag. Maury thought that an evening of all female voices would lack variety. To his credit, I think Mario Fratti was intrigued. I was *sure*. There is a time in the creative process when *right* becomes *might*. A strength comes over one, and the lights brighten. But my collaborators turned them out on me and withdrew their material. No way were they having this outrageous idea pervade their material. For two weeks I was not on the project. Maybe they were looking for another director/choreographer, maybe they would rather have not done *Nine* at all than to agree to my concept, maybe . . . maybe . . . I don't know. I wasn't present. After two blackout weeks during which I was surprisingly calm and clear—if it was to be, it *would* be—I got the call.

"We've decided to give it a try, just for the workshop." We completed the cast: Liliane Montevecchi was to portray the producer, a rich French woman who carried a revolver in her purse; the gondolier, a beautiful young woman with long blond hair wearing a sarong; Raul would double as the priest; the Germans at the spa were now four buxom fräuleins; and the opening number, conducted by Guido with baton in hand on a podium was called "Overture della Donne" (Overture of the Women), with each actress on her own individual white tile pediment and arranged about the stage like an all-female orchestra.

It was magnificent to hear and see. Maury had created a beautiful collage of themes from the score, and they all sang joyfully like perfect angels, a male chauvinist's dream of heaven. Then the trouble in paradise begins, and Guido loses control of his heavenly harem. *Nine* won the prize for Best Musical of 1982. Maury

*Tonynight '82. Top, with Liliane Montevecchi.
Bottom, Ann Miller, me, Ginger Rogers,
Milton Berle, who presented me with the
Director Award (and a kiss) and Liliane who
won a Tony, too, that splendid evening.

won for the score, I won for direction, and Liliane won a Tony, too! Thanks Liliane, you were my inspiration.

Now back to *Grand Hotel: The Musical*. I went along with Jack to hear the score. Both Bob and Chet are senior members of the race and are chock-full of fascinating stories from the show business wars. What full careers they've had, including one of my favorite musicals, *Kismet*, for which they adapted the music of Borodin, adding poetic lyrics: Their songs sing themselves in the throats of vocally gifted performers. This time out they'd written their own music, and I liked it very much.

Green as I always seem to be, I pass this autumnal-colored advice on to any potential director or interested theater devotee: Always consider the source. In this case it was this pair of elderly gentlemen—Chet playing his piano and Bob singing in his sturdy, yet tortured voice—presenting their new score to me with such feeling and devotion to the art of songwriting that I was deeply moved. I miscalculated how these songs might sound in the voices of an actual cast. Rehearsals began, and song after song faltered while struggling to soar out of the characters' mouths.

I've always known that I have a weakness for composers presenting their songs. There is a passion invested in their personal renditions that springs from the creative source. It is most compelling: Jerry Herman singing "I'll Be Here Tomorrow," Cy Coleman singing

"It's Not Where You Start It's Where You Finish," Marvin Hamlisch doing "What I Did for Love," Dick Sherman of the Sherman Brothers team singing "Supercalifrag-ilisticexpialidocious." Chances are you haven't had the pleasure of hearing these particular renditions per-formed on the living room grand piano without the trap-pings, but with all the *heart* in the world. It doesn't get better.

Then comes the reality of putting on the actual show and the constant assessment of what works and what doesn't, and a large portion of *Grand Hotel* wasn't work-ing. Let us skip through the tedium of at least two years of meetings with the authors to get the rehearsal version of the show in order. Let us skip the endless backers' au-ditions and casting sessions and arguments and laughs and stories—theater people tell great stories—and meetings with designers, producers, press people, ad-vertising people, union people, and on and on. Let us skip to the opening night in Boston.

Bluntly stated, the show didn't work. With the excep-tion of the choreography and the physical trappings, the show was deadly. What to do? Well, one step at a time. One could have pointed the finger anywhere at this rav-eled tapestry and said this needs severe attention. I pointed to Liliane Montevecchi's song first. She was now playing the ballerina, the role Garbo had played in the movie. I felt that if I could get her story right, which I felt was at the center of the piece, then maybe the rest would fall into shape. A new song was needed pronto and, as the director, I ordered the new material from Wright and Forrest.

One day passes, no new song. Second day passes, no new song. On the third day I arose and went to them for the song. They weren't ready. Well now, I'd been vamping with the cast for three days, "shoveling the shit" it's called in common parlance, or "rearranging the garbage"—you can brush it off, repaint it, relight it, but it is still garbage. I needed new material, and we had one and a half weeks left to get this turkey in the oven. Mr. Bob Wright said, wagging his finger at me, "Don't hurry us. Johnny Mercer said, 'A couplet a day.'"

"A couplet a day!"

I'm almost certain that the great lyricist of "Moon River" didn't have a flop multimillion-dollar Broadway musical out of town in Boston with less than two weeks to go when he said that. He was probably out in La-La Land sitting in the sunshine before the cameras were even rolling for *Breakfast at Tiffany's*.

I went directly to the producers and said, "I need help." They said, "Get it." I called Maury Yeston, my former composer/lyricist of *Nine*. He said, "I'm getting in my car now, I'll be there by curtain time tonight."

He was. By the end of the week we had a title song, a song for the ballerina that fit like a glove, and a new number for the ingenue. Quietly, Peter Stone had come in to fix the book. I had the help I needed, the cast had their hope restored, and the original writing team had a bite on for me that's never abated. So be it. I did what was necessary to save the patient, and an ailing show became a hit.

The week we opened on Broadway the Berlin Wall came down. *Grand Hotel* was set in 1929 Berlin just before the stock market crash that brought about the Great Depression. How's that for synchronistic coincidence?

I hate it when it gets ugly on a show. It always does though, and you've gotta be hearty to survive. If it's not the writers, then it's the producers or the cast. There is always turmoil, but if you're lucky some good can come of it all. I have always tried to be kind to everyone, but please don't mistake my kindness for weakness. "The play's the thing."

* There's a saying in the biz that goes, "The only good playwright is a dead playwright." I don't believe that. I would much rather be struggling to create a new show with all the accompanying fights, than reinterpreting an old one. There's a certain safety net one has in doing revivals—you know you've got something even before you start rehearsals—but I greatly prefer the quest for the new, the unknown. What are we saying with this show? What's the beginning? What's the middle? What's the end? Let's change this, it isn't working. Let's change

*that* and make it better. Let me try a choreographic sequence here that could cover the next ten pages of story
without a word. Could you write a song for him, letting
us know what he wants? Can you write a song for her,
giving us her back story? Could the last scene go on a
bit longer and give us a chance to realize that what
they're saying is not what they mean? Show us that
they're leaving each other but yearning to stay together,
if only. . . .

That's the stuff that dreams are made of, and making
a new show is making a dream come true.

I've had severe wrestling matches with writers and
producers through the years, but I'd like to believe that
when I hear a good idea I recognize it as such and in-
corporate it into the proceedings. Mike Nichols says,
"The best idea wins."

I have one notable exception, for which as a direc-
tor/choreographer I still kick myself. Peter Stone, at the
request of the producer Pierre Cossette, wrote a book
musical with Cy Coleman (music) and Betty Comden
and Adolph Green (lyrics). It was entitled *Ziegfeld Presents Will Rogers*. I thought the title was leaden, unmusi-
cal, and arrhythmic. The search was on for a new one,
and after much deliberation at zero hour it became
*The Will Rogers Follies*, a terribly flat title, I think. Earlier,
in passing, Adolph Green asked me, "What about calling
it *Will-a-Mania*?" which was the title of the opening
number.

In my dead head I heard a lyricist pushing his lyric

and not a wise and experienced showman, which he is, naming a play. I let it slip through the cracks, and all these years later I'm still sorry. It's always better to live your life without regrets.

Even with an unimaginative title, *The Will Rogers Follies*, starring the wonderful Keith Carradine, won the triple crown: the Tony Award for Best Musical, the New York Drama Critics Circle Award, and the Grammy. Cy and Betty and Adolph won for the score, and I won Best Director and Best Choreographer. Peter Stone, the man who created the whole shebang, was passed over. We would have had nothing without him. I try to have no regrets, but it's hard sometimes. I regret that Peter Stone didn't receive his due; he is one of the world's last remaining librettists.

If you have a child, encourage him/her to write librettos for Broadway musicals. They'll have no competition; the field's wide open. I think Broadway's wide open right now, too, a blank stage waiting for something new to encourage our saddened spirits to soar. It seems that little on the musical front is really happening now—just revival after revival, rehash after rehash, warmed-up leftovers, the occasional anger-based social criticism show set to music, but no exciting, entertaining new cuisine. No joy. No entertainment.

*With Keith Carradine on opening night of *The Will Rogers Follies*. When he didn't win his Tony, he quietly said to me, "Tommy, it would have been good for my career to have won, but it's better for my soul to have lost." Keith Carradine is proof positive that angels walk the earth.

I've always likened putting on shows to cooking, perhaps that's because my father and mother both used the kitchen superbly—Mom was a baker and Dad a cooker. Both Gracey and I grew up without fear of the kitchen, and some of my favorite hours on this planet have been spent gathering ingredients and preparing meals for people I love. Jane Curtin says, "The family that sautés together, stays together." Cooking with my real or surrogate family is a primary source of entertainment for me.

Believing this, perhaps that's why I sometimes wear my chef's attire to rehearsals. In making shows, we're simply cooking up food for the spirit, nourishment for the soul. The shelves in the store seem to be almost barren of fresh fixin's these days, but one can somehow always scrape together a meal for the hungry. I feel there is still a great appetite for musical theater if we could just encourage the growth of a new crop of thinkers. I feel the lack of writing talent starts first with our educational system, then with the fact that a heady living can be made on television serving up fast-food sitcoms each week, and, finally, with the existence of only one proper newspaper in New York for intelligent review of our new theatrical offerings. There used to be a whole bunch of theater-loving critics stationed at our New York dailies, and a mixed bag of reviews stimulated the theater-going public to see and judge or enjoy for itself. As one daily publication after another folds we are left with one legitimate source, which has been given an all-powerful po-

*Gene Kelly in his final public appearance presenting
me the Pinnacle Award. Here's what he said, "Just
about every other generation someone comes along and
revivifies and revitalizes the American musical theater.
This generation that someone is you, Mr. Tune. All
of your colleagues admire your artistry, skill, and
professionalism, but we admire more your gentleness
and kindness to the talents with whom you work.
God bless you, Tommy Tune."
He does. God bless you, Gene Kelly.

sition. That is not healthy for the present and future life of Broadway theater.

I've noticed in the film world that some very, very fine work has disappeared in its initial release only to be found and celebrated later on video. "How could we have let that one get away?" we exclaim with wonder as we view exciting work on our home VCR? Which brings us to the very essence of living entertainment—its value and its sadness. When we perform in the "false" mediums (television, cinema, recordings), we are saying, "I am here." And that's a good thing. But in the theater we are saying, "I am here *with you*," and those last two little words make a crucial difference.

"*With you*, I am here *with you*," and neither of us will ever experience this time again in our lives. Tomorrow night my show may be giving another performance, but you won't be here so it will be hugely different; or if you do come back it will still be hugely different because all the other members of the audience will not be the same. My idea of a fine occupation is to do the same show night after night until the technique of the performance is so ingrained that one is free to soar with the belief that whatever happens the foundation is solid. A long run becomes a launch pad that allows one to spring higher each time the curtain rises.

However, it's a living, breathing event that can last only as long as someone comes to experience it. If no one comes, it ceases to exist. If we stay home and watch *Court TV*, then this theater event will close, never, never

*What an honor! Gwen Verdon inducted me into
the Theatre Hall of Fame. Here she is giving me the
Michelangelo Award. In her presentation speech
she called me, "Ultimum optic to the max." I saw
her in *Sweet Charity* fourteen times. She was
ultimum optic to the max—and then some.
I love Gwen Verdon.

to be seen again. A fine theater performance is a precious jewel, but not one that can be placed in a gold setting to be taken out, admired, and worn to a snazzy party. Theater is, in essence, perishable—fresh food to be served up for tonight's dinner. So eat. Nourish yourself. Clean the platter. If the event is worthwhile, entertaining, and enlightening, then you can move it, like a treasure, like fine furniture, into the apartments of your mind, and there it can dwell forever.

I have some great treasures upstairs in the apartments of my mind—Zeffirelli's production of *Lady of the Camellias* at the Winter Garden; Anthony Newley in *Stop the World—I Want to Get Off* at the Shubert; Carol Channing in the original company of *Hello, Dolly!* at the St. James; Mike Nichols's production of E. L. Doctorow's *Drinks Before Dinner* at the Public; Zoe Caldwell in *Master Class* at the Golden; Gwen Verdon in *New Girl in Town* at the 46th Street Theatre (now the Richard Rogers); Jessica Tandy and Hume Cronyn in *The Gin Game* at the Golden; Tom Stoppard's *Arcadia* at the Mitzi E. Newhouse; *A Chorus Line* at the Newman (Public); *Amadeus* at the Broadhurst; *Pacific Overtures* at the Winter Garden—the upstairs apartments are crowded, but there's always room for one more piece. May I always be receptive to a shimmering three-dimensional experience in the theater that speaks to our time and to all time, that is so specific that it is universal, and that entertains and enlightens and makes me feel glad to be alive.

* As a kid my summers were spent on Grandma Tune's Oklahoma farm. She and her girlfriend, Aunt Rose, lived in the "big house," an ancient three-storied gray wooden Victorian structure that had seen better days. It was slightly racked and spooky, and I loved it. Years later when *Psycho* came out, that house that Norman Bates and his mother occupied looked just like Grandma Tune's Muskogee residence. There were big fields of various crops surrounding it, and long rows of corn separated it from the "little house" that belonged to Aunt Bob and Uncle Fud (her real name was Fanny and his was Beauford, but those monikers were never used).

Mom and I slept each night in their house but I'd take off each morning as early as possible, crossing the fields to Grandma's. Each summer the corn crop was high enough to hide me, so in between the rows on those Muskogee mornings, I found room to dance in private to my heart's content. If I didn't get too carried away I could still make it to Grandma's in time to catch Aunt Rose doing her hair. Now that was a sight to behold.

Grandma was a big pioneer woman who looked a lot like an old Indian man and a little like Gertrude Stein. Aunt Rose, however, was a tiny bowlegged little critter, not unlike Mammy Yoakum in the *Li'l Abner* comic strip, except that she always wore a proper calico housedress, black lace-up shoes, and thick flesh-colored woolen stockings. Her hair had never, *ever* been cut and came down to her calves. If I timed it right I could sneak a look at her brushing it before she quicker than a wink twisted it into a tight little knot right on the top of her head. Brush, brush, brush, lickety-split, and it was up! I'd miss this ritual a lot of mornings though because of my cornfield choreography. It was a difficult choice to make but I loved dancin' and kickin' up that red Oklahoma dirt in those rows of corn.

Opening night of *Nine* on Broadway fell on Mother's Day. Maybe the collective consciousness in the theater that night helped bring back my memory, but I suddenly straightened in my seat that magical evening and realized that I had arranged all those women onstage like rows of corn and that the formations they danced were exactly like those I'd patterned as a child on Grandma's farm. This realization bowled me over, causing me to laugh and cry simultaneously. I thought to myself, "The corn was as high as a chorus girl's eye" (sorry, Oscar). One's life, one's work, it's all one thing. If I'd spent less time choreographing and more time studying Aunt Rose I might have been a hairdresser.

---

* In a state of elation I called Betty Comden a few years ago with exciting news.

Betty's voice, singing on her answering machine, "New York, New York, it's a helluva town. . . . Please leave a message."

"Betty, it's Tommy Tune. I'm so excited, I just got a booking in the Catskills. I'm going to play Kutsher's."

She called back, "Tommy, you've got it *backwards*. You're supposed to *start* in the Catskills and work your way *up* to Broadway." That proves to me I don't care where I play—in the cornfields, on Broadway—I just love show business.

For the performance in the Catskills I dressed in my hotel room rather than in the dressing room provided me, which was located in the kitchen at Kutsher's. I usually work in a set of white tails and to risk a collision with a waiter overloaded with a tray full of bowls of borscht . . . get the picture?

I was duded up in my costume and tap shoes heading surreptitiously toward the showroom when the elevator opened on a female New Yorker. She braced herself with her hands placed on either side of the parted doors, took a big inhale and started, "Mister Tune, you're my biggest fan—" I suppressed my laugh. She continued, louder, "I get down on my hands and knees and *kiss your feet!* Your *Grand Hotel* was positively . . . *underrated!*"

She floored me with that one. I was crying with laughter, holding on to the walls. I limped to my backstage position, still heaving, and pulled myself together, but when the overture began I cracked again. The tympani hit, and my conductor Michael Biagi announced in his basso-profundo voice, "Ladies and Gentlemen, Kutsher's proudly presents Broadway's one and only,

T-o-m-m-y Tune!" I entered in tears. God, I love to laugh!

Then I got a Las Vegas booking and immediately called Carol Channing.

"Carol Channing, how do you play Vegas?"

Without a beat she responded, "Tommy Tune, you start with the finale and go *up* from there."

Good advice. I was a hit in Vegas, and Siegfried sent me two dozen red roses with stems longer than my own. Wow!

✱ In the early seventies I was dancing in the chorus of a show entitled *How Now, Dow Jones* at the Lunt-Fontanne Theatre. George Abbot was the director and Michael Bennett had taken over as choreographer. He gave me a featured spot in a newly minted number, and we threw it in on a Wednesday matinee during our preview period. Working with Michael Bennett was a privilege. We'd kill ourselves for him. In turn he'd give us so much confidence that we became fearless, a great feeling to have onstage. The new number seemed to work, and the very next morning I got a call from the casting director Alixe Gordin.

"I'm casting the movie of *Hello, Dolly!* to star Barbra Streisand and to be directed by Gene Kelly. Roger Edens and I saw you yesterday in *How Now, Dow Jones*, and we want to fly you out to Hollywood for a screen test. Have your agent call me."

\* On the backlot at 20th Century–Fox doing the
"Dancing" number from *Hello, Dolly!* with
Barbra Streisand, Michael Crawford, and the
late Danny Lockin. The film musical, I wonder if
they'll ever make them again. A lost art?

What agent? I didn't *have* an agent. Chorus boys didn't need agents, and agents didn't need us. We only made ninety bucks a week back then and what's 10 percent of that? I've never been good with math but the answer is, not much.

I called an agent I'd heard of, and he smelled money. I begged our producer, David Merrick, to let me miss the Monday night show. He reluctantly agreed, and I was flown to Hollywood, first class—put up in a beautiful hotel, rehearsed, made up, costumed, screen tested, directed by Gene Kelly—WOW! Tuesday I was back in the dressing room at the Lunt. Was it a dream?

Three weeks later a knock on our dressing room door, "Hey, Tune, it's for you!" Outside the door in the dingy fourth-floor hallway stood Peter Cereghetti, the agent, who said with a grin, "How'd you like to go to Hollywood and make a movie?"

I stepped back into the dressing room, stunned. "They tested twenty guys and I got the part!" A whoop went up from that Broadway team as if I'd scored a touchdown. One of ours had made it! And the fact that I was to be paid $750 a week became legendary. That I was to be signed to a seven-year contract with 20th Century–Fox was beyond belief. I performed that matinee performance of *How Now, Dow Jones* two inches off the floor. My featured spot was cut from the show three days later, but who cared? I was off to Hollywood.

Broadway chorus boys' dressing rooms are like locker rooms. After all, like football players or basket-

\* "You can take the boy out of the chorus but
you can't . . ." I'm the tall one on the end
doin' the "High Hat" number from *My One
and Only*. I love playing on a team.

ball players or hockey players, we're a team paying the bills with our bodies. Wearing our uniforms, sweating heavily, we put ourselves in physical peril eight times a week, definitely blue-collar work, but with notable perks—the lights, the music, the dancing. Chorus boys' dressing rooms are also riddled with humor: sarcastic putdowns of the stars, "Is it just me or does she have a rhythm problem?"; cynical world-weary observations about the writer, "Let's chip in and buy him a pair of scissors"; about the director, "Is it spelled P-A-C-E?"; about the top soprano, "Maybe a tuning fork would help." Complaints about choreography and costumes and dance shoes and rehearsal hours abound, all hurled out with a great knowing comic edge. Once I was elevated to my own *private* dressing room I really missed the chorus camaraderie. During the *Busker Alley* tour when I'd get lonesome, I'd pack up my makeup and move into a corner of the boys' dressing room. A bunch of guys in the same boat can really make you laugh. I love the concept of teams.

✱ After the *Seesaw* tour in the late seventies, with no job prospects except the Milliken show, an industrial musical fashion show held each year at the Waldorf-Astoria which paid extremely well, my performing career careened into a cul-de-sac. Salvation came in the form of

*What I did for dough. In 1972, dressed for the
high-paying Milliken Breakfast Show. In 1992
I was named to the Top Ten International
Best Dressed Men's list. Obviously the voters
never saw me in this get-up.

scenic designer Robin Wagner, who had designed *See-saw* and has had tremendous success with his many other Broadway designs, including *A Chorus Line*, *City of Angels*, and *Victor/Victoria*. Robin recommended me to the poet Eve Merriam. She called and described a theatrical idea to me.

"The piece I envision is set in a Bostonian gentlemen's club, 1907. The members plus a page, a maestro, and a black butler gather for drinks and good times, telling hoary old jokes and singing songs about women. The material, all authentic songs and jokes of the Victorian era, is particularly demeaning to the female sex. They laugh and drink the night away and as the sun comes up they drunkenly make their way home to their wives. All the men will be played by women."

"Well, that sounds interesting. I've always felt anybody that's any good can play any part, but since the cast is all women, what part could I possibly play?"

"I want you to direct it." Pause.

"OK, great, but where did you get the idea that I could direct?"

"From Robin Wagner."

I would like to formally thank Robin Wagner for giving me my directorial career. I have no idea how he knew I could do it and neither does he. There is a lot to be said for intuition.

*The Club*, as it was called, came at a time when feminists were just getting started. The bras had just been burned, remember that? Women who weren't simply toys for men or trophy wives were walking about with their breasts swinging and their armpit hairs growing and demanding to be seen as human beings.

Now, I'm not a feminist, or a sexist, or a racist, or a masochist, or a sadist, or any other kind of *ist* except an optimist, but the idea of *The Club* intrigued me as a *showman*, so Eve and I set to work. Eve wasn't a playwright, but she was a fine poet, and I just loved her.

We started with a pile of Victoriana, and together we fashioned an evening. The gents arrive one by one at the club, each having his own presentation by the page and his top hat, cane, and cape removed by the butler; drinks are served, and the evening's festivities begin. As Eve and I ran out of steam I had the idea that they rehearse the Annual Spring Frolics, so at one point they scramble offstage and return in drag much like a Victorian version of *The Hasty Pudding Show*. The big difference, of course, which made the minds of the time spin, was this: Here were women, spending their evening as men, and then showing up as men parading as women. It was a real sexual doublebind, extremely controversial, and a big hit.

Martin Gottfried, the theater critic and author, wrote a definitive review of the proceedings proclaiming me the new director in town. The limos arrived with the old guard, the Off-Broadway crowd came and with them the intellectuals, the homos, and the lesbians—oh what a sight the nights were down there on Bleecker Street, and what diverse reactions! Cheers, boos, ridicule,

*The gents of *The Club*,
Algy, Freddy, Bertie,
and Bobby.

solemnity, hilarity, praise, outrage—it made one male friend of mine queasy to the point of nausea. *The Club* was a Rorschach test for the sexually unaware, the sexually aware, and the sexually confused! And what did it do to me? Every show I've ever been involved in has colored my perception of the world—the intense work that creating a show involves cannot but help affect the central core of your being—and if it doesn't then it's simply not worth doing.

*The Club* certainly changed my view of the world of the sexes. The original cast, Eve, and I took the journey of discovery to heart and soul, seeking the answers to such questions as What makes a man? What makes a woman? What is the difference between the two? Of course anatomically women are "open" between the legs, and men are "closed with fruit." After the extremely obvious is recognized, everything else becomes mysterious, and the quest for the solutions were serious and hilarious. We moved into Edith Wharton's decaying estate in Massachusetts called The Mount. We had our separate rooms, but as our rehearsal period progressed we became so close and loving that after dinner, pajama clad, we'd migrate to the big carpeted living room, hover near the wood-burning fireplace, put our pillows in a circle, and sleep/dream in our new-found fraternity.

One day we were all packed in our broken down excuse for a van seeking out a restaurant on our dinner break. We stopped out front of what appeared to be a possibility. I slid out of the car in my summertime cutoffs and tank top to check it out. As I headed up the path to the front door this huge whoop of laughter erupted from the "gents" in the van. Minutes later, "OK, they'll serve us dinner, but before you get out of this van I wanna know what you were laughing about—what'd I miss?"

It turns out that as I strode up the walk, being viewed from behind, Marlene the page had said wistfully, "Oh, gosh, if I were a woman I'd want to look just like him." Pause. Gales of laughter as the realization of sexual confusions locked in.

I hope this somehow suggests to you the depths of our quest. None of us who undertook the show ever quite saw the world the same way again. In fact, there was a bond formed from those many years ago that lasts today, and there is a reunion annually of "the Gents" of *The Club*. Of course, I'm not invited—I was never a member. One had to be open to belong—I'm closed with fruit.

---

* Do you ever feel like you're in a foreign film and the words you're speaking have been translated literally into English, and as a result the syntax is all upside down and backward, and the verbs have ended up at the finish of the sentence, and instead of saying, for instance, "rays" of sunshine you have chosen "spokes" of

sunshine like in literally translated Italian? The result is something like a strange pidgin poetry, affected and distant and not of or pertaining to whatever it was you were trying to express. Does this detachment thing ever happen to you? It's like the whole scene has been underscored with some distant largo movement from an obscure symphonic composition, and you've been dubbed!

Today in physical therapy my German trainer said very calmly in his accented English, "You are not hard enough, working-sweating, you should be by now. Squeeze together the buttocks."

"Peter, I'm working as hard as I can."

"No. You should be sweating; it's important. Imagine you are in white tights in a follow spot dancing for thousands and it is your own five minute solo and you have diarrhea. Now squeeze harder your buttocks together."

You know what? It worked. I squeezed harder my buttocks together.

After a lengthy road tryout of a new musical, *Busker Alley*, with only one week to go before our New York engagement, something highly unexpected occurred. With one minute to go in the Sunday performance while doing the final reprise of the title song, I slipped onstage and broke my right foot. In that one musical beat, doing a step I've done at least a thousand times, the whole future of that show changed. It makes one realize just how vulnerable we are as we tightrope walk through our performances eight times a week. I break my foot, and two hundred people are put out of work. The backers lose their multimillion-dollar investment, and my career is in tenuous balance once again. Rumors fly in the press: I'm faking it because the show isn't any good and I don't want to bring it in (which makes me a coward in my eyes). I'm gravely ill and dying (which I'm not, but then the fact is "We're all dying, Otto"—that's my favorite line from *Grand Hotel*). I've been paid to take the fall so the producers can collect on the highly publicized hefty insurance policy they'd taken out on me with Lloyd's of London (interesting angle since I'm told that Lloyd's, as I write this tonight, is trying to get away without paying *anything*). These are just some of the tall tales circulating, all completely untrue and all of dubious origin.

The truth is I broke my foot onstage in the line of duty, being the best Broadway soldier I know how to be. Someone said there are no accidents. If so, then I'm still looking for the reasons behind this nonaccident that befell me. It's a shock to be dancing to the extent of one's capacity on one beat in the music and then not dancing at all or not being able to dance on the next.

What an odd, debilitating sensation it is for a dancer to suddenly not be able to dance. A bird with one wing, a horse with two legs, a tree with no roots. My whole dancing body went into trauma from the abrupt finale it suffered. What is a dancer who no longer dances? Gwen Verdon said that dancers die two deaths: one, when they stop dancing, and two, when they stop living. I

\* Ready, set, stop! Under the *Busker Alley* marquee.
When this photo was snapped I just couldn't
believe my misfortune. Our producers, Fran and
Barry Weissler, had commissioned Leroy
Neiman to paint my likeness on the façade of
the St. James Theatre in magnificent colors,
and here I stood, broken.

spend two hours every day on tortuous machines invented by a man from Transylvania, driven to the
aching point by a fierce German instructor with little
mercy but great knowledge of the workings of the human body. Then I undergo an hour of physical therapy
on just my foot, followed by an hour of floor barre with
Zena Rommett in which we duplicate the standard ballet exercises that are normally done vertically. We do
ours on the floor with our bodies horizontal. The weight
has been taken off our feet and legs, but the conventional rigors remain in our prone position. This is a brilliant technique and I hope it will be my salvation. It has
been six months since the accident, and I have yet to
dance a step in that time. I honestly don't know if I shall
ever be able to dance again, although not to be able to
dance is unfathomable to me.

"Why did this happen?" I continue to ask myself,
which I know I should not be asking. Acceptance and
patience and determination are the bywords in this new
year that spreads out before me. I suppose I'm what
would be classified as a bad risk now because of what
happened in that one beat of music. I wonder if I will
ever appear in another show. Will I ever get another
chance? Is this phase of my life over? Will there never
be another "half-hour" call in my future? When 5:00
P.M. rolls up on the clock face, will my dancer body ever
again start to bristle knowing that in three short hours
I'll be up there onstage in front of an audience doing
what I was born to do—dance?

I never really understood what dancing is and how I do it. What causes my body to make the shapes and moves that constitute a piece of choreography? Agnes de Mille said dancing was "nonutilitarian movement set to music," but I need to discuss that with her. How does she account for one of my favorite ballets, *Moves*, by Jerome Robbins, which is performed to silence?

What a mystery dancing is to me. How do the images in my head travel through my neuromusculature and come out of me in rhythmical physical phrases? How does it differ from walking, or running, or skipping? Someone asked Barbra Streisand once how she held her notes so long without breathing, thus making her aware that she was doing something extraordinary and causing her not to be able to do it again for months. She told me this herself many years ago, on the set when we were filming *Hello, Dolly!* Gene Kelly was our director, and he gave me the best direction I've ever been given. He simply came up to me between takes and said, "Tommy, dance better." And I did. I wonder if I ever will again.

This is really a major ponder for me tonight as I write this. What shall I do with the remainder of my life? Of course, I can direct, but dance has always been my central source, the point from which my other gifts have flowed. Without that core where would I be? Where am I? I've never realized how important dancing is to me until I am denied it. Is it that way with love, too? I think so.

"God, I'm a dancer, a dancer dances," sings Cassie in

*Before the fall.

*A Chorus Line.* "Ye who danceth not knoweth not what we are knowing," says the Bible. Martha Graham says, "Dance is the landscape of the soul." To answer Freud's question, "What do women want?" John Updike concludes, "Women want to dance." Well, this man does, too.

The sun is appearing over the East Side buildings, it's morning, and I've written through the night. It's January 3, 1996, and in a few hours I'll be in the studio starting the therapy process all over again. So—"To sleep —perchance to dance."

∗ Warning: The next eleven paragraphs deal with intimate sexualities. If you don't want to know, skip 'em and pick up with the story about Josephine Baker.

∗ For our first night in Tokyo, our employers, the Takarazuka Revue Company, had reserved an expensive two-bedroom suite in the Hilton Hotel for my collaborator Jeff Calhoun and me. It was well appointed, spacious, and cost 1,500 smackers a night. Calhoun discovered that just by calling the front desk at any hour one could have a massage within minutes. We'd been on the plane for eighteen hours and were pooped out.

"Let's do it."

He phoned. Sure enough, ten minutes later two little

Japanese women arrived in what looked like oriental nurse's uniforms with their pocketbooks over their arms. They could have been schoolteachers. Jeff and I had hastily showered so we were both waiting in our hotel robes in the central parlor that connected our bedrooms. Off he went with his gal and I with mine.

Since they didn't arrive with massage tables, I headed for the bed and started to remove my robe. This action was greeted with a flurry of excited sounds and protesting gestures. "Oh, I see, so sorry, I'm supposed to leave my robe on?" Nods and bows and Japanese sentences followed. I stretched out on the bed on my stomach, she climbed up, and the service began. Through the cotton robe her little fingers pressed and probed, shiatsu style—no direct contact with skin, but antiseptically comforting after the long flight. After the shoulders, arms, and legs, she finished up the dorsal part of the treatment by using both hands and rocking my buttocks back and forth at least fifty times. I was starting to get a rise out of it, like when you ride in a bumpy truck for a long time, all the jiggling causes a reaction. If you're a guy reading this, you know what I mean; if you're a girl, just believe me, it happens. Now it was time to turn over for the frontal massage. She espied my hardened condition under my robe and then for the first time looked at my face. "Ah," she exclaimed excitedly, "you, movie star. You, movie star."

"Well, actually I, uh, made a couple of movies a while ago but I wouldn't say . . ." It was obvious she didn't understand a word I was saying. I trailed off, slightly embarrassed by my physical predicament.

"You, movie star. You, movie star."

She leaned in closer, her hand covering her mouth; little giggles followed, little murmurings, little gestures toward "it"; more giggles, little nods—finally, *finally* I got the message. For a few more yen, another service would be provided. Sure, why not, agreed, whereupon she disappeared into the bathroom for what seemed like half an hour. What preparation this? Costume change? Props? Who knew? Then the distinct sound of sheets of Kleenex being pulled from the box—one, two, three, whuff, whuff, whuff, four, five, six—and over and over, at least three dozen times.

She returned with a veritable Mount Fuji of tissues clutched to her breast and proceeded to build a moat around my exposed manhood. It now looked like there was an ice cream sundae on my crotch with the tip of my dick as the cherry on top. She then unbuttoned the top of her uniform and, placing my hand on the left mound of her padded bra—thwok—she got down to her task. What technique! Using just her thumb and her index finger she proceeded to make little up and down strokes, jerking, quite steadily, quite fast, quite short— push-pull, push-pull, push-pull.

Well, it was just *awful*. I felt like I was being masturbated with a pair of rubber tweezers. I closed my eyes tight and tried to think of other things. Anita Ekberg. Bodies of water. Trains in tunnels. My hand still resting

* My Moscow debut in the revered Hall of Columns.
I'm tap dancing on the exact spot where the
Russians had laid out Lenin, but no one seemed
to mind. In fact, the response was sensational.
This was before perestroika, and I don't think
they'd ever seen tap dancing before.

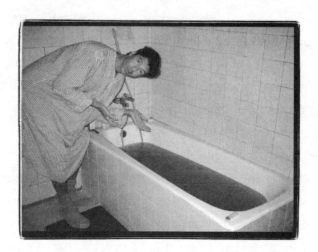

* Later, in the "official residence," my response to
the water wasn't sensational. It was brown. Dark
brown. As much as I loved the Russian tour,
on returning home after a rough twenty-one days,
I got down on my belly and kissed the ground
of America. I really lucked out being born here.
Freedom is *not* just some people talking.
It's tangible.

on the mound of foam was not content. My fingers slowly moved up and over, crawling inside to feel a little flesh, for God's sake. Oh no, not permitted—a little slap on the back of my hand, and it was replaced onto the foam.

Oh God, this is terrible. The poor Japanese men who have endured this torture. Hey, maybe they like it. I'm thinking, "What am I gonna do? It will be so insulting to her if I don't complete my part of the deal, and at this rate we could be here all night." Cut to the chase. I *could* be the first guy to ever *fake* an orgasm. Grabbing the mound of Kleenex and covering myself, I rolled over on my front and made terrific moaning sounds accompanied by the appropriate thrustings. I'm a good actor. I pulled it off. Her uniform rebuttoned, yen exchanged, pocketbook over arm, little bows, and she was gone.

Calhoun wasn't offered the extra treatment, and till this day I don't think he believes what happened to me. But it did. It's the truth. "Movie stars" visiting Japan, beware!

* I won the Josephine Baker dance contest at the Palace Theatre one New Year's Eve and ruined my Hollywood career because of it. I have no regrets but the story may interest you. Here it is.

It was New Year's Eve nineteen seventysomething. I

was heady with the first rush of success. *Seesaw* was having a substantial run at the Uris Theatre (now the Gershwin), and I was being celebrated by critics and audiences alike for my performance in the production. I had two great second-act musical numbers that literally stopped the show. All in all, it was a high time for me, because in addition to the show I was in a relationship that really worked, living in a top-floor loft on Fifth Avenue and 17th Street called Giraffe House and loving life the way small children do under the tree on Christmas morning.

I believe I'm historically accurate in saying that I was playing the first openly gay, major role in a mainstream musical comedy on Broadway, and I was the first long-haired, character juvenile to dance across the hallowed hetero stage boards in "sunny openness," as John Simon wrote. This wasn't calculated on my part at all; I was completely naive, which is probably why it worked so extremely well. Michael Bennett, my mentor and close friend (and the director of the show), may have seen—and probably *did* see—the bigger ramifications of this innocent showbiz indiscretion, and perhaps he was liberating some aspect of himself through me. He served me up with congenial tones for the Broadway audience of that time. I know it was a first that had no cringe factor, like you would have if a homosexual cartoon character had been dropped into Walt Disney's *Bambi*, if you can imagine such an inconsistency.

At any rate, with the Cy Coleman score and the best

choreography I've ever created—under Michael Bennett's tutelage and with his encouragement, of course—I was the toast of *my* town, if not *the* town. What a time!

I feel like the old actor in *The Fantasticks* as I bring out my yellowing newspaper clippings for your perusal. I'll divert the praise from myself by praising the writing technique of Walter Kerr, my favorite critic of that era—no, not because he loved me, but because he loved the theater and expressed himself in print with theatrical élan matching, and many times improving upon, the images concocted in whatever show he was reviewing. Walter opened his review of *Seesaw* thusly:

> In what may be the nuttiest, and maybe just plain funniest number I have ever seen in a musical, dancer Tommy Tune of *Seesaw* uses his supple heron's legs to summon on stage a chorus in blue hats and vast mantle of balloons, spins them about the stage in a crack-the-whip exuberance that makes them seem lighter than their lighter than air clothing, climbs a staircase made of balloons beneath a chandelier made of balloons, and in his irrepressible idiocy, keeps calling for even bigger and bigger finishes. The finishes finally get so big that the floor seems knee-deep in confetti, whereupon Mr. Tune is handed a broom from the wings, and ordered to clean the whole thing up. He is still very happy as he sweeps that last litter, and the last lone dancer away.

* Me and Baayork Lee on our toes in *Seesaw*.

And while I'm at it this from the *Toronto Star:*

> Midway through the second act of *Seesaw*, at the O'Keefe Centre, a bountifully gifted dancer-singer named Tommy Tune (really) seized his chance.
>
> The audience, hitherto present at a rather conventional musical, was suddenly made aware of someone out of the ordinary. If *Seesaw* had been going anywhere, Tommy Tune could be said to have stopped the show.
>
> The most stylish, charming, talented, not to mention tallest person on the stage, Tommy Tune had an irrelevant but divine number called "It's Not Where You Start (It's Where You Finish)," an extravaganza with a billion balloons, confetti, white staircase, top hat, and the dancer's own endless legs.
>
> Tune, the most lyrical and witty male dancer to appear at the O'Keefe all year (no, I'm not forgetting Nureyev), raises *Seesaw*'s spirits to stratospheric levels.
>
> All of which makes Tommy Tune very welcome. He plays the dancer's gay friend, and gives the role an honesty and gentleness which support our response to his performing genius. In repose or on taps, high stepping or saying goodby, this is an exceptionally affecting performer.

This really looks like bragging but, hey, I'm from another country called Texas. It's our gross national product!

It was announced in the paper that Josephine Baker was opening her engagement at the Palace Theatre with a special New Year's Eve performance. Having only heard of the legend and never having seen her, I knew my chance had finally arrived. It was a lickety-split dash from the Uris Theatre, following our *Seesaw* curtain calls, to the Palace through the blocked-off area of Times Square that New Year's Eve, but Michel Stuart and I made it in time for the dimming of the house lights. As we slid into our seats, a tall, heavily perfumed black man in a turban and white caftan—it could have been Geoffrey Holder, but it wasn't—passed up and down the center aisle flamboyantly passing out bouquets of red roses with the whispered command, "These are for Josephine. Throw them on the stage for her. Let's cover her in roses."

"OK," I think to myself, "It's probably a tradition." The crowd was older and permeating faded elegance. They'd probably seen her in Paris in their youth and had come here tonight to recapture a romantic memory. The overture started. An ancient conductor with tired wings flapped his best dwindling tempos as the second-rate, under-rehearsed band waded through a medley of her songs. The effect was slightly soiled and tattered, but it had a bygone charm that accelerated my heartbeat. The bored musicians struck up her most enduring hit, "J'ai deux amours—mon pays et Paris" ("I have two loves—my country and Paris"), and those in the know started to scream, "Josephine, we love you." The flowers were catapulted to the stage—I followed suit—and voilà, Josephine appeared, stage left, preceded by two Borzoi hounds on rhinestone leashes.

Dressed in a red velvet and chinchilla design by Erté, including fur muff and towering Russian-style hat, she was a legendary vision. Standing ovation, cheering, applauding—all of which truly confused the canines. One headed across stage, the other spun on itself several times and headed back to the wings. Already slightly unsteady on her high high heels, Josephine was being pulled in opposite directions and simultaneously being pelted with the flying roses. The band wound down. She couldn't seem to get the hand mike to her mouth because of the skittish dogs. The crowd sat, and she said, "Oh, dear!" Then referring to one of the hounds, "Just like a woman, she has a mind of her own and won't behave herself."

The dogs were really tugging now—clearly they were not Josephine's dogs, but a pickup pair for this special evening's entrance. It's gone wrong, and now, through her failing eyesight, she espies the floral tribute at her feet. "Oh, dear!" she whimpers. "How can I step on these posies—it would not be right to step on such beauty—can you clear them off for me?" Silence. Nothing. Several beats pass. We chuckle uncomfortably. "Hello back there. Can someone help me?" Finally, a T-shirted and dirty khaki-clad stagehand arrives in a surly mood with a push broom and parts the way for her toward center stage.

She makes a few opening remarks and introduces a male flamenco dancer who takes over the stage as she slowly retraces her steps to the wings. The poor guy is left alone to stamp out his rhythmic tattoos midst the roses. What a mess! The evening disintegrates from there, spiraling downward.

Josephine has no help at all, and she is struggling gamely to put on a big show. Costume change after costume change, there is nothing to hold our attention but this limping excuse for an orchestra with Bar Mitzvah arrangements. At one point she appears on a motorcycle, looking impressively trim in a rhinestone-studded denim jacket and jeans. She was wearing a short wig, and the effect was youthful/old and tough in a sort of French ou-la-la way. "OK, boys," she exclaims, "tonight let's turn the Palace Theatre into a *beeg deescotheque!*" The recorded thump-thump came out through the speaker system, and she started clapping her bejeweled hands together, encouraging the audience to do the same. It wasn't working. Back to this scene in a moment. Stay with me.

As my personal success with *Seesaw* grabbed hold a lot of offers rolled in, mostly mediocre, but one extremely significant.

A team of producers who had enjoyed great success on Broadway and had now widened their field to include the movies called with an attractive deal. They had just produced an Academy Award–winning musical film and were keen to strike again while the iron was still hot. They had developed a screenplay, which was delightful, and when they saw me onstage in *Seesaw* they knew they'd found their star. With the studio resources available to them, a lucrative deal was drawn up and agreed to. My favorite clause promised a trailer dressing room for the location shooting that specified a ceiling tall enough for me to actually stand while getting into wardrobe. That might not sound like an extravagance to you, but to me, it was like having a suit that truly fit instead of one that was marginally short, which was "de rigueur" for those days before I could afford proper tailoring. The prospect of starring in a film and in a *musical* film, at that, produced by savvy showmen who'd already proven they knew how to make that tricky form work on camera, was dazzling to me. This was my big break because everyone knows that being a true star means being a movie star. Ask anyone who struggled up from the stage or television, or the record industry, or stand-up comedy clubs—a true star equals a movie star, and my time had come.

Back to Josephine.

"Come on up and dance weez me, we make beeg deescotheque on Palace stage deez very New Year's Eve," invited Josephine. She actually sounded like she had a French accent. I suppose all those years abroad had taken their toll on her native St. Louis speech patterns.

Not an old soul was stirring in that nostalgic crowd. "Come on! Come on!" she entreated.

I couldn't let her die up there another moment. I stood up and took the long walk down the center aisle of the Palace Theatre up the little set of jury-rigged steps, and there I was face-to-face with Josephine Baker in a blazing follow spot. Since I was, by then, the new boy in town appearing in the latest musical, I was recognized, and the audience applauded enthusiastically. Josephine didn't know who I was from Adam, but at least I was a warm body. She smiled. The sight of her close-up was a shock to my young eyes. These were the days before plastic surgery was as commonplace as the 7-Eleven, and hers had been done by an amateur, stretched and pulled and wrapped, twisted, and tucked. It might have been those "lifts" they used to use that were glued to the cheeks, then the attached strings were pulled tight over the head and tied off. Then "plunk" goes on the wig, and there you are. The effect was formidable, but just the beginning of a bizarre, almost psychedelic, experience.

We started to dance vis-à-vis. Flashing disco lights started whirling. Unimpressed with my presence but surprised by the reception and by my extreme height, she did a big take, kind of held her face, and reeled backward in a comically exaggerated gawk. It got a huge laugh, and she turned to the crowd and invited more couples up to her disco stage. "Come on! Come on! Don't make me dance with this thing *alone!*" (A bigger laugh).

The ice was broken. Down the aisles they poured, and soon the stage was peopled with a varied assortment of characters all "thump-thump-air-fucking," which is how that kind of dancing has always looked to my choreographic eyes.

My job done, I hastened to retreat down those rickety stairs to return to my seat, but no—Josephine had something else in mind. She was turning the affair into an old-time amateur dance contest, wherein the host holds a hand over each contestant and the audience applauds; the one getting the loudest claps wins. I won and remained onstage for my reward as the rest of the group headed back into the house.

"Wait, Wait!" she said exiting, "I have a prize for you that I brought all the way from Paris!" Awkward stage wait. She returned with a small gift-wrapped package, and as she presented it to me there was huge applause. She was baffled. I remember her saying, "I don't understand this but you are definitely the beeg winner!"

I got back to my seat, mortally embarrassed, and opened my New Year's-winning prize. It was a pair of silverplated Swank brand cufflinks, tacky, wonderful, given to me by Josephine Baker "all the way from Paris"—via Canal Street. I treasure them.

The critic reviewing the evening in the next day's paper with cruel, disheartening, washed-up descriptions told of the tall man in the caftan and turban, that "sashaying, sentimental camp follower," and in the same paragraph mentioned me by name, thereby suggesting that we were one and the same—a flamboyant drag queen come to pay homage to his gay icon. The big boys in the Hollywood studios picked it up and called the producing team. They in turn called me, saying, "What in the hell did you think you were doing last night? You've caused a big problem for us out there with the guys in California. I mean they kept it quiet about Cary Grant but he wasn't ever dancing around in drag onstage with Josephine Baker!"

"But Ernie!" I said, "I wasn't in drag! I've never done drag! I was up there helping her out!"

"Well, it doesn't sound like that in the paper!"

"Read it again, carefully," I suggested.

Never mind. The deal dissolved. Not overnight, but by subtle lessening degrees, and then one day it was invisible, like it had never happened. I wish I could say that the movie was made and mention the title, and you would recognize it as a delightful hit film that So-and-so starred in, and that So-and-so is now a big Hollywood star; but I can't. That movie was tailored for me, and it never got made. And I never became a movie star. But at least I won the Josephine Baker dance contest!

A few years ago I broke my *left* foot, the *other* one, during a minor earthquake. I was in a Hollywood hotel, missed the last tread of a staircase, and the break curtailed a tour of my one-man show (plus thirty) called *Tommy Tune Tonite!* Carol Channing read of the accident and called me in New York. She herself was laid up with a broken leg in California, and we laughed and turned our misfortune into something better as we do when we chat. Three days later a huge box of Chinese

\* My big break in Tampa. The doctor called it
"A nasty one," as he applied the cast. At least I got
a lot of attention from (*clockwise from right*)
Phillip Oesterman, Jeff Calhoun, Naikes
Constantino, and David Warren-Gibson.

healing herb remedies arrived from her. I took them religiously as did she on the opposite coast, and we both healed in time for our next performing engagements.

When I broke my *other* foot, my *right* foot, in Tampa—the exact same bone but now on the other side—and was laid up in my bed in Florida, who was the first to call? Carol Channing.

"Well, doggone, Tommy Tune—did you break that doggone foot again?"

"No, Carol Channing," I said, "it's the exact same bone as before but on the *other* foot."

She took a pause, I heard an intake of air, and then she said, in her inimitable fashion, "Well, perhaps it's God's way of giving you symmetry!"

Carol Channing is the best, and here she is again in this book. She once told me I had the eyes of her father. Maybe that explains this strong connection between us.

Around the same time as the Josephine Baker debacle, I made another naive misjudgment. A press agent for the New York Dolls, a popular rock group, called in a panic. The Dolls were performing on Halloween at the Waldorf-Astoria, and part of the evening's festivities was to be a costume contest judged by Ben Vereen, who was starring in *Pippin* at the time. A death in the family had made his participation impossible and would I replace him? Yes, of course. Halloween has always been my favorite holiday—all those spirits hovering, all those altered states that people assume because of the funny costumes they're wearing. Since I was standing in for

Ben Vereen I naturally chose to go as a Harlem Globetrotter. Well, it seemed natural to me.

I started with the head. I buzzed up my friend Judy, who is the same race as Ben, and asked if I could borrow her Afro wig for the event. She loved the idea and agreed to help me get the other disparate parts together. We had to work fast. Being a "disappointment act" isn't easy, and it had been advertised on a full page in the *Times* that Ben was a judge along with Tammy Grimes, the fashion world's Chester Weinberg, Texan Rex Reed, and I don't remember who else. Bruce Steier loaned me some striped satin basketball shorts, I already had the sneakers and athletic socks, and out of nowhere appeared a tank top with the number seven. Stein's Dark Egyptian greasepaint provided just the right skin tone—falling somewhere between Ben and Judy—and I was set. I must say I looked really handsome with dark skin—no wonder white people are always seeking suntans. Deep-colored skin accentuates the eyes and mouth and teeth. I looked tall, skinny, but cute in my Globetrotters uniform—on with the Afro and out I went.

I carried a basketball as an accessory and literally stopped traffic as I exited the stage door that night. Flashbulbs popped like crazy as I entered the Waldorf, and I ended up in *Time* magazine. Now this was way before political correctitude, but even then my appearance created a scandal. As I write this, I swear I meant no disrespect, and lo, these many years later, when Ted Danson in blackface appeared with Whoopi Goldberg at the Friars Club it was simply history repeating itself. I know he meant no disrespect either. I *know* this, but let the media get a handle on it and watch what happens!

When we lose the ability to laugh at and enjoy our differences—in fact to celebrate them—what an angst-ridden world we become. Tiptoeing around on eggshells is not a comfortable way to perambulate through life. It seems repugnant to giggle at the difference between the sexes much less the difference between the races. Because of this I feel the world is a pressure cooker without a release valve—no opening to let the steam out. Laughter at ourselves and with others is that release valve in our culture, and it is being stifled. It will cause another civil war. I feel it. It's just a matter of time. We can't keep the lid on much longer.

As a nation we've lost our sense of humor because it's being censored—how else can we explain the success of Howard Stern? He has the nerve to be reactionary in the most extreme and vulgar manner possible, and people are saying yes to him because our natural instincts for laughter are being stunted. Our freedom. Go, Howard. And who's doing this to us? Smug talking heads sitting behind anchor desks on the boobtube? Poison-pen scribblers in printed publications blatantly lacking in journalistic scruples? Editors of tabloids approving unresearched half-truths for sensational effect? Our judges—our media judges. We should get them for the Halloween costume contest. Don't mind me, I'm just clearing a blockage. Maybe it isn't proper to *black up* these days, but it certainly wouldn't hurt to *lighten up!*

Down home in Houston I lived an extremely segregated existence, not only from Blacks, but also from Jews. There were no Jews allowed in our neighborhood. Isn't that shocking? It is to me now, but not then—it was simply the way of the world. Jews *were* allowed in public schools, however, and somehow—not knowing exactly what Jewish or Gentile meant—I gravitated to this wonderful girl named Carole Anne Byers, her friend Betsy Bloom, and later to Martha and Betsy Kaiser. I even attended Freddy Gerson's Bar Mitzvah. My father used to ridicule me with the line, "Bubba and his Heebs, Bubba and his Heebs" (short for Hebrews).

Then an amazing and fortunate life-changing event occurred. We moved into a brand new beautiful ranch-style house. After living there for about six months a family moved into the newly completed house next door. I don't know how the Krost family got around the strict segregation laws, but they did and became my second family almost instantaneously. This huge-hearted Jewish family opened my young eyes to a whole new world of menorahs and chopped liver and gefilte fish and borscht and "oy vey" and "gevalt" and "kvetch," and I just loved them so much. Gracey was the flower girl in their son Stan's wedding—the only "shiksa" in the wedding party at the synagogue. And then a miracle happened. Dad shifted his position and came 'round, growing to love and adore the Krost family. We were all so happy being neighbors. What good fortune in having an adopted Jewish family at that time, that formative time, in my young life. It gave my narrow existence a whole new dimension. Since then I have naturally gravitated to and embraced these talented, laugh-loving, outgoing, and wonderful people. It appears easy to dispel the bugaboos of prejudice—religious, racial, or sexual—through love, but I know it's not. I just got lucky in my little world and in the little world of show business, too. Take away the Jews and there's no show business; take away the Blacks, the homosexuals, lesbians—likewise I'm sure. Show business is just a microcosm of the world. Let's mix and celebrate. Life is like a really good show that's never lacking in variety.

* New Subject. Generation Xers, punks, baby boomers, listen up!

In the sixties we were called "the Beautiful People." My girlfriend Roberta, dressed in her own unique style, and I, fresh from Carnaby Street in my navy blue full-length maxicoat, were passing through the glamorous lobby of the Dupont Hotel in Wilmington on our way to the theater when we overheard a woman in reverential hushed tones say to her husband, "Look, Harold—there go the beautiful people."

Harold snorted, "Looks like a beanpole to me." Beauty is in the I.

Opening night of the musical *Double Feature* in New Haven, high above our heads on the "ankle stage," a long narrow letter-box-shaped proscenium stacked atop the theater's regular proscenium, the dancers were revealed only from the knee down, and a beautiful dance I'd choreographed with Thommie Walsh drew huge laughs from the audience. A few days before, we'd unveiled it to our director Mike Nichols and he had wept at its beauty.

He came to me consolingly, "Oh, Tune, they laughed at your beautiful work." "Oh sure," says I, "I learned a long time ago when I'm at my most serious I am my most hilarious." That seems to be a leitmotif in my life. Many times, when I am completely sincere, people think I'm completely phony. When I think I'm really funny, people are offended by my comic take. When I'm embarrassed it's mistaken for arrogance, and, yes, when I'm serious people think I'm kidding. Earlier, before the performance that night, Nichols had introduced me to Lillian Hellman. She said, "Mister Tewnnne, your reputation precedes you." Well, I liked that. Let 'em laugh. Let 'em cry. Be true to your vision. Beauty is in the I.

I love to please, probably too much. At this point in my career, I'd be a better artist if I'd just do what I do, trust the gift, and express the individual within. I can't control the way the work will be received. To try to anticipate critical reaction stifles creation. Work with a pure heart and a clear mind, ask for a state of grace, and hit it!

*You mean Tommy Tune's not in "Tommy" at all?*

＊Phillip Oesterman called early this morning to remind me of this important anniversary in our lives.

"Happy St. Patrick's Day, Bubba. Thirty-three years ago today we arrived in Manhattan, remember? You got a dancing job that very day. How's your foot?"

"Colorful." Actually it was throbbing. But I didn't want to talk about it.

The hours we've spent on the phone have really logged in by now. Except for my daily talks with Phillip, I don't speak on the phone unless it's absolutely necessary. Why do I need to talk on the phone when I have this running commentary of ceaseless chatter babbling in my overactive mind? Lordy, Lordy, my telephone talks with myself use up a lot of units. As much as my brain carries on one would expect that I would be brilliant by now just by virtue of exercise alone—not so. Although the file is full, the longer I live the less I know.

Thirty-three years in New York City this anniversary morning could perhaps bear some examination. Look what Jesus accomplished in thirty-three years, and here I sit with no Sermon on the Mount to my credit, no feeding of the masses with one loaf of bread, no carpentry skills—although I have been crucified by the press, but that's not exactly a personal accomplishment and certainly doesn't serve as an example for all humankind. No, my one real accomplishment in these thirty-three years is simply to have survived—body intact, heart in shards, but still here.

Renaissance man thought the purpose of living was

"to see the vision of God," and here I am celebrating mere survival. And yet, one flip through my Rolodex and every other name seems to be that of a deceased person. I don't take their names out of my Rolodex when they pass on. Their phone numbers and addresses are no longer valid, but seeing their names where they've always been serves to remind me of their continued importance in my life. Besides, as the casualty list grows every day I find it hard to remember who I *knew*. At least it's easy to remember who I *know* these days— very few indeed. Is Francine LeFrak getting married again? I seem to remember an invitation to her wedding but that was just before the cruise. Did I R.S.V.P.? Francine was such a supportive producer on *My One and Only*. She kept bringing me Ella Fitzgerald recordings of Gershwin tunes hoping to improve my vocal renditions, I suppose. Also quite unusual for a producer, she kept begging me to add more people to the cast as if volume might cover up our shortcomings. I did and I guess it worked. The show was a hit. Thanks, Francine.

* Warning—the next seven paragraphs deal with intimate sexualities. If you don't want to know, skip 'em and pick up with the story about *Busker Alley*.

∗ "You were behind on the bell kicks again, but it was a great performance. Can you believe that audience? We're really a hit now." It was Baayork Lee, dance captain extraordinaire, talking in my little dressing room off stage left. "Oh, this is Brick, I snuck him in, he loved the show."

Brick was tall, raw boned, wide shouldered, dirty blond. He grinned the grin that didn't want to show his teeth. Baayork could always find them or maybe attract them like some kind of electromagnet. They were always handsome—extremely handsome—in a variety of colors, in awe of show business, and broke. Did she *keep* them? I doubt it. They never lasted that long.

"I gotta give some notes to Twiggy and she won't be dressed yet. Is it okay if Brick stays here? I'll be right back." And she was gone.

I was in my long white terrycloth robe direct from the shower. My hair was still dripping, and I could feel the rivulets of water slide down my clavicle, forming a pool that spilled over and ran down my chest. My dressing room chair was from the barbershop scene in act one that was cut in Boston. It was huge, had a footrest, oversized leather arms, and a padded brass headrest. I had revolved it to greet Baayork, now I sat facing Brick as he continued to grin. His back was against the door, and he pushed it closed with his butt—click—not locked, just shut. His grin slacked. A drop of perspiration had formed just under his nose and was taking the long slide down the U-shaped gully leading to his mouth. I gotta say I wouldn't have minded being that drop of sweat traveling slowly downward and arriving at that perfect pair of lips. They were full and pink and tan and they started to part ever so slightly as he moved the three feet across the tiny room to stand as close to me as possible. I was jacked up high in the barber chair so we were vis-à-vis, only the footrest keeping us separated. He straddled it, one sneaker to the left, one to the right. With his index finger he touched my "third eye" and ran it down my nose under the tip to my mouth, down my chin, throat, sternum, arriving at my navel. Staring intently and mischievously into my eyes, he loosened the terrycloth tie. My robe fell open. I was totally erect by now—he leaned over me at just the right angle, formed those cushioned lips around me in a tight circle and slowly wet-slid down the shaft. Without a hitch he arrived at my pubic bone—his mouth clanked ever so slightly against my body, and then a strange thing happened. Nothing. He just stayed there. Not a move. I could barely sense his breath. Ten minutes passed, I grew harder and longer. I felt bigger than the room. I was swollen in ecstasy. It was unendurable. I didn't make a move; he didn't make a move. Absolute stillness prolonged. "This is the sexiest encounter of my life," I thought. Red to purple to spires of acid green— then to white, no, what's whiter than white? Light. That's it. White light. Liquid. It poured out of me. I felt my life pouring out of me, convulsing, gushing, but in complete stillness. Circles within circles. Coming and coming. This is a menopausal musing of a mythic fuck, and it never happened at all.

"Wanna go with us to Joe Allen's?" Baayork was back, her "Chock-full-o'-notes" composition book under her arm.

"Thanks, I'm joining Liliane at Sardi's. Nice to meet you Brick."

His sexy grin widened finally to a smile. He was toothless, and I never saw him again.

* I can hear the St. Paddy's parade on Fifth Avenue far below my penthouse perch—distant drum cadences and brass melodies rise and fade. My broken foot seems to be healing, each day the pain is less. I'm finding the courage to walk. Dancing, of course, is another matter, and I'm not ready for that yet. Patience is an exercise in . . . patience.

I read in the paper today that the producers of *Busker Alley* have not paid the ad agency for the work they did on the show before its aborted New York opening. The article says the reason the show was canceled was because "Tommy Tune broke a little toe." *A little toe!* They surely can make you sound like a wuss. A broken little toe, and I've had several, has never caused me to miss a performance, much less to cancel an entire production. Being a dancer is being an athlete, and sometimes you lose a season. I've been very lucky that I haven't lost more.

\*With Ophie in our penthouse perch.

A chorus of bagpipes makes an aural crossover far below on the avenue. It sounds like the sun is out, but it's not. It's a gray, cold day, but the spirit of the city is shining. Spring is just days away, and the scent is already in the air. The first days of spring in Manhattan are worth the price of the entire freezing winter. Woolen scarves are thrown off and smiles that haven't appeared throughout the cold season are suddenly on everyone's faces.

We didn't have four seasons in Texas. Houston offered two, and both were damp. I remember the first time I dried myself in New York after a hot shower and found that it actually worked. Amazing! In Houston, pre-air-conditioner Houston, one never got entirely dry, ever. I grew to love the scent of mildew from my closet mixed with the night-blooming jasmine outside my bedroom window, the attic fan gently rumbling, bringing in the wet, warm air all through the night. Home—is there ever anyplace like home? Thirty-three years here in New York and I still feel like I'm visiting, partly I suppose because I'm always on the road. As soon as a show I've directed and choreographed has opened on Broadway I book myself for a performing tour. It's a touch with the reality of show business that I crave. When you're directing, you're observing life, but when you're performing, you're participating. Directing is maturing; performing is youthening. It's the difference between sitting in the park watching the children play and actually getting up and playing with them. A steady diet of both promotes balance for me. I recommend it, in whatever form you wish to find it. Observation. Participation.

Here's a recent observation. As a working man in the theater, when I observe marginal work being lauded by the audience and critics, a demon rises up inside of me and screams, "Not good enough—not good enough!" and I wrestle him down, tagging him "the Jealousy Dragon." But I've misnamed him, because when I observe superior work in the theater he doesn't appear at all. When it's so good that it leaves me in the dust, that I marvel at how it was ever conceived and created; when I give way all my grumpy, critical judgment and return to the childlike wonder; when I'm sitting there laughing one moment and weeping the next; then I know I've tasted the remarkable, and my Jealousy Dragon evaporates into the *astonishment* of it all. This has finally happened for me again recently. An unlikely musical, *Floyd Collins*, at Playwrights Horizons theater on 42nd Street, fulfills on every level. In the beginning it's a tough love. A man gets trapped in an underground cave and unsuccessful rescue attempts are made. Is this the stuff of musicals? A resounding *Yes*. In the hands of inspired creators—direction and book by Tina Landau, music and lyrics by Adam Guettel, set, lighting, costumes, sound, orchestrations, cast—it's perfection realized. Inspiration granted. Back to the drawing board.

Knowing that inspiration flows from many sources, I always seem to work best when I am creating specifically for someone I care about. This individual person becomes a kind of muse for me, and the work I perform becomes a kind of direct service to this individual, ultimately spreading out to an entire audience, should all go well.

One example is an early success, *A Day in Hollywood/ A Night in the Ukraine*, a musical doubleheader, which opened at the Golden Theatre to surprisingly rave reviews and the delight of audiences. It had a healthy run.

My inspiration and reason for taking on the assignment was its producer, a grand gentleman of the theater and impresario, Alexander H. Cohen. My first Broadway job, dancing in the chorus of a musical adventure of Sherlock Holmes called *Baker Street*, was produced by Mr. Cohen. Also in the chorus and my theater dressing-roommate was Christopher Walken, who has gone on to huge success in Hollywood. People forget he was a terrific dancer first. Root talent.

Alex Cohen was so kind and generous to each and every one of us in the cast, I believed that that was the way all of Broadway would work. I remember in our out-of-town tryout in Boston there was a severe snowstorm, and our cheap hotel, the Avery, which the gypsies dubbed "the Ovary," was several blocks through the "combat zone" from the Colonial Theatre's stage door alley. Alex and his partner/wife Hildy Parks commandeered limousines for the whole company and shuttled us back and forth nightly. Imagine this green chorus boy taking his first limo ride from the stage door of the best theater in the country to the cheapest hotel in Boston. If there had been a hotel doorman his jaw would have dropped. As it was the local hookers, pimps, and other residents of "the Ovary" were baffled: "If that kid can afford a car like that why would he stay in a dump like this?" The night clerk started calling me "Mr. Tune." That was a first, too. I think, for about two weeks, I got kind of spoiled. In fact, Alex Cohen, spoiled me for every other producer who's followed. He just did it all with such magnanimous flair.

Years later he'd had a run of big flops on the Great White Way, so when he called to ask his ex-chorus boy to direct and choreograph this nifty little show, *Hollywood/Ukraine* . . . yes, I was flattered, but quietly in my secret heart I said, "Make a hit for Alex!" I set about gathering the team: Thommie Walsh as choreographic partner, Wally Harper for musical direction and arrangements, Michel Stuart and Donna Granata for costumes, Tony Walton for sets, Beverly Emmons for lights, and a cast that included David Garrison, Peggy Hewett, Priscilla Lopez (who won a Tony for her performance), Frank Lazarus, Stephen James, Kate Draper, Niki Harris, and Albert Stephenson. Jerry Herman joined us in Baltimore during our less than successful tryout period and wrote three songs that pushed us over the top. Through it all I was making a show for Alex, out of respect, affection, and a desire to "repay his kindness with interest." It became selfless work, which is always the better way.

＊Niki and Albert dancing on the "ankle stage" high
above our heads in *Hollywood/Ukraine*. Below,
I expose how we did it—extended slow-motion leaps,
impossible feats of balance, reverse spins—all effected
with the aid of horizontal poles that were hidden
from view on Tony Walton's splendid set.

\* More pole dancing, vertical in *Busker Alley*,
horizontal in *Grand Hotel*.

Warning: This "do it for someone you care about" syndrome can get you in trouble sometimes, altering your ability to emotionally distance yourself from the material at hand and make impartial value judgments on all elements involved. Such was the case with my unsuccessful production of a play with dancing entitled *Stepping Out* by Richard Harris.

I was in London with Eric Schepard, my mentor, friend, agent, and the man who literally created and gave me my career. Eric died of AIDS on my birthday several years ago, and I have been rudderless without him. His root talent was dancing, and his agenting grew out of his on-the-job training as a chorus boy on Broadway. Extremely handsome as a young man, he was the possessor of an open personality, which I think was his secret way of compensating for the fact that he was illegitimate and to my knowledge never met his father. Eric was one of those rare breeds of agents—one who understood the "show" as well as the "business"—and was never content to let a "deal breaker" contract clause impede the forward movement of a show in which he believed. "You're gonna take less money, Tommy, and have a show—10 percent of something is better than 15 percent of nothing." Eric never let me mount my high horse. He'd knock me off on the way up every time with a hilarious and compassionate kick in the butt! God, I loved him, and I miss him so. He handled some very fine talents and was as famous as an agent can be before he ever welcomed me into his stable. It was my performance in

*Eric Schepard, the man behind the man.

*Seesaw* that called me to his attention, and we hit it off instantly. We never had a bad word or opposite opinion. He knew and I knew, and our paths were in sync. Except once, and that wasn't his fault, it was mine.

In London we attended a West End matinee performance of a minor play that had had a spectacularly long run, and we were very moved by it. It was a tale of losers who met once a week in a church basement to learn tap dancing. We learned of their extremely simple and complicated lives through these weekly tap sessions, and in the end they gave a charity performance for friends and relatives where they rose to the occasion and did their very, very *limited* best. As the group danced their pitiful choreography to the nth degree—it was a routine to "Stepping Out with My Baby" by Irving Berlin—I looked at Eric and he was weeping, and I realized I was looking at him through a veil of tears of my own. We decided, then and there under those emotional circumstances, to do the American production. A grave error. Never decide on business affairs under the influence of high emotion. Always make business decisions coldly, then give your heart to the project and awaken the warm feelings that your good humanity possesses.

The first thing to go wrong was that the show was to be a coproduction between the Nederlanders and the Shuberts, the two rival clans of Broadway at that time. Liz McCann, our producer, brought the two houses together; I was amazed that she had been able to pull the deal off. Later their philosophies clashed. One side loved bus advertising, the other thought it was a waste because certain buses, once outfitted with our ads, remained parked in the garage for weeks on end. One side was computer oriented and could predict trends, the other studied surveys and weather reports. One liked subtle poster design, the other preferred the David Merrick red and yellow school of show art. One said, "Let it run and find its audience," the other said, "Close it." But there was a lot more conflict, too.

Although the show had played for years in London, Irving Berlin suddenly would not give our Broadway production the rights to use the title song. This problem didn't present itself till we were fully cast and well into rehearsals. Yikes. Through the entire evening we watch the characters toiling away to "Stepping Out with My Baby" as they improve from complete nondancers with feet of clay to a galvanized and heart-warming group of earnest tappers giving their all on their big night of triumph. Suddenly we were out of a title song—a *famous* title song. I should have stopped right then and there— my inner voice told me to do so—but we were already promised and left with nothing to do but press on.

I'm not good with "plan *B*s." We substituted another song, I don't even remember which—that says something, doesn't it? Then Tony Walton, after a long and constructive design meeting, suddenly pulled out. I should have stopped then and there. "Well, surely you're not gonna cancel a whole production because you lost your set designer!" Then Ann Roth, the costume designer, had to pass the assignment on to her assistant due to a time over-run on a movie to which she was committed. I should have stopped then and there. But we had our cast, and we had our theater and surely. . . . It just doesn't work that way. *A* does not replace *B*. *A* is *A*. And *B* is something else.

After a painful pregnancy, *Stepping Out* was stillborn. I was doing this show because of Eric's tears. Watch out. Agents aren't supposed to cry! So I had my first flop. Up to this point I was the golden boy of Broadway. Everything I touched was blessed with phenomenal success. The chain was broken.

When you break a piece of prized porcelain you can put it back together with Krazy Glue, but the crack always shows. Or you can choose another method of repair. Someone suggested that the pieces can be soldered together with gold, and the imperfection can take on a new dimension enhancing the overall beauty of the whole. I would like to believe that this is the path I've followed in patching together the remnants of my life.

The tiny details and minutiae of *Stepping Out*'s characters gave me keen insight into the lives of the staff and guests inhabiting and working in the *Grand Hotel*. Not having slaved away in detail with *Stepping Out* would ever have prepared my eye and heart to handle the multiple stories we brought to the stage in *Grand Hotel: The Musical*. There is a Japanese saying that goes:

一日一日　が　昨日　の　積み重ね　です。

"Ichinichi, ichinichi ga kino no sume kasani desu."

Which means, "Each day, each day is the student of yesterday."

In America we say, "Experience is the best teacher."

I need more.

* In the fifties it was de rigueur to get a car for high school graduation or at least a gold pen and pencil set. I asked for a trip to Broadway. My parents consented, and I am eternally grateful. I stayed at the Algonquin Hotel and rode up to my room on the same elevator as Anna May Wong. Wow! I called my tap dancing teacher, Camille Long Hill, who'd actually *been* in New York, and asked her what to do next.

"Go out the front door of the Algonquin and turn right, Tommy, then keep walking and you'll get to Broadway."

She was right, but before I got to Broadway I came to the Belasco Theatre. It was really hot in New York that summer, and the side doors of the theater were ajar. Most theaters weren't air conditioned in those days. Imagine! I peered in those vertical openings and saw real actors (among them Arlene Francis) with real scripts in their hands, walking about a maze of folding chairs, which represented the set, and I thought, "Golly, that's just how we do it when we're putting on a play down home—it's exactly the same." I was truly amazed that the process for professionals was equal to the process for amateurs, and now, through experience, I know that there is no substitute for the work, the toiling, the struggle, the time.

One of my favorite memories on this subject involves Tony Walton. We were having our last rehearsal before the opening night of *A Day in Hollywood/A Night in the Ukraine*. The cast was onstage, I was standing in the center aisle of the Golden Theatre; I was dancing, they were dancing. We finished. We made "Circle." I'm a big believer in Circle and have been ever since I was introduced to it by my high school drama teacher Ruth Denney. Before every performance Ms. Denney instructed us to join hands in a big circle, thereby literally connecting the cast members into one divine human form. She'd have good words of positive encouragement to say to us, and if there was a weak link in the chain it would be strengthened. I've continued making Circle since high school and have found that it really works to align a cast. It's so specific. After Circle, during which we expressed our joy and good fortune at being able to be working in the theater and our excitement and nervousness in anticipation of the opening performance, which would be happening in less than four hours, we wished each other "Good show" (it's bad luck to say "Good Luck," peacock feathers backstage are taboo, and never wear yellow on opening nights) and dispersed. The cast headed to their dressing rooms while I went out the center aisle to the Golden Theatre's lobby

*Outside Joe Allen's with Ruth Denney, my high school drama teacher.

*Moments before the opening night curtain of *The Will Rogers Follies* with the cast in the Palace Theatre's basement doing what Mrs. Denney invented, Circle. Cynics, listen up, it works!

and into the street. On the back row of seats lay a small *flat*—a piece of scenery for the second act—and hovering over it in the semidarkness was our set designer Tony Walton with a tiny brush and a small can of scarlet paint carefully outlining the edge of a minuscule detail. Hours later that piece of scenery made its debut in a Broadway show. In the theater there are no substitutes, there is only the real work.

In Alexis Smith's dressing room in the Colonial Theatre minutes before the opening of *The Best Little Whorehouse in Texas* in Boston, I remember sewing a button on her second-act costume. It needed to be done. I did it. In the theater there are no substitutes, there is only the real work. And as Mies van der Rohe said, "God is in the details." My costume design teacher in college, the one and only Lucy Barton (she wrote the book, *Historic Costume for the Stage and Screen*), said that in the theater there was no need to use colored thread, only black or white, but not to mistake that for lack of attention to detail. Detail and superstructure become even more important for stage costumes because of the "magnified eye" of the audience, not to mention the wear and tear that a stage costume must endure, but surprisingly, the color of the thread doesn't show. Oh, what a character Lucy Barton was. Her lectures were true master classes in theater, even when she would often drift into whole lengthy passages in French. Some brave soul in the back of the room would venture a hand raise to rout her from this Gallic barrage: "Miss

Barton, you've gone French again." Pause. Getting back on track she'd be heard muttering under her breath, "Language cripples!"

Also on campus at the University of Texas at Austin was the leading authority of the age on Shakespeare, B. Iden Payne, a highly knowledgeable and articulate devotee of the Bard. Rumor had it he actually "knew" Shakespeare; he was also a no-holds-barred eccentric. The role of the old actor in *The Fantasticks* by Texas alumni Tom Jones and Harvey Schmidt was based on Mr. Payne. All but declared legally blind, Mr. Payne could be spotted on his office balcony, heavy thick-lensed glasses in hand, silently staring directly into the Texas sun. When it was suggested that perhaps these ex-tended periods of sun-staring might be of further detri-ment to his compromised eyesight he shot back that it was "the *only* thing that keeps me seeing at *all!*"

Dress parade for *A Winter's Tale* was a rare scene, what with Mr. Payne and his failing eyesight situated next to Miss Barton on the first row of the theater, and the actors teetering on the edge of the forestage in blinding white light. Miss Barton, who I neglected to tell you was aurally compromised, wore her hearing aid nested in a halo of fluffy Colette-like frizz directly on top of her head. Iden, his binoculars pointing up at the play-ers on stage, saying, "Lucy? Lucy, who? who?," and Lucy next to him saying, "Iden, Iden, what? what?," were a pair to behold. We likened them to Sid Caesar and Imogene Coca in a sketch they might have done on

*Your Show of Shows*. However, Lucy's eye and Iden's ear for detail were unerring.

Mr. Payne was a stickler for this one exercise that matched vocal exactitude with perfect expansive gesture. It went:

> The great Earth,
> The vast sky,
> Yon distant star,
> I reverence you all.

We were made to do it over and over till we attained the perfect vocal nuance and the heightened accompanying move.

Years later I was preparing for a lecture I was giving on the cruise ship *The Royal Viking Sun*. We were out in the middle of the China Sea on a perfect morning. I was on B Deck warming up my voice and body, and it seemed the perfect moment to recall Mr. Payne's exercise. I started: "The great Earth"—I looked down, and there it was flowing beneath me as far as I could see; "The vast sky"—above my head, and expansive beyond belief; "Yon distant star," and indeed one lone bright star was left over in the early morning sky, still twinkling, magical. I suddenly got what Mr. Payne was trying to impart. With overly dramatic but sincere tears streaming down my face I executed the extravagant bow that ended the sequence. "I reverence you all," and I did. I think I got the hang of it finally—the God in the details.

＊ I don't think a day has passed in the last fifteen years that I haven't contemplated suicide. Have I been in a state of severe depression for the last decade and a half? I don't think so. I believe I'm picking up on a male zeit-geist that is of epidemic proportion just now. Life has become a lot harder for guys than for gals—of late or maybe for always. I don't know. We *do* know that women live longer. Is it because they don't have the bur-den of rising to the occasion each time sex beckons? Does this penile action wear us down to an early grave, or is it the marketplace and our inability to cope with stress, or our ability to cope with it so well—as in stuff-ing it deep down inside—that causes the premature fi-nales? I know that statistically the suicide rate for guys is growing at a remarkable rate, and the suicide rate for women has plummeted. Hmmm.

OK, maybe I'm just trying to attach my own private demon to a bigger movement that doesn't really exist at all, just so I don't feel so all alone. I know that suicide runs in my family; I already told you about my paternal grandfather. Well, add three aunts to the suicide statistic and an attempted one by my sister, and that seems to be a rather bottom-heavy scale for one family. Maybe I've inherited the suicide gene. I think people who know me may be surprised by this information—in fact, as I write this, it's a revelation to myself.

Then there's the method to contemplate: I live high in the sky with a great terrace; skydiving is possible. They could say my act "went over well," but the splat would be so messy—and yet that short abbreviated sensation of flight is very seductive indeed. Various slicings or shootings are possibilities. One of my aunts used a hose with steel wool lodged in the end of the exhaust pipe of her Chevy and then secured the other end of the hose in the rolled-up car window. Inhaling the fumes, I suppose, was a gentle exit because when we found her she didn't look at all agonized. In fact, she'd neatly placed her white platform sandals on the passenger side, her spectacles on the seat beside her, and just simply rested her head on the steering wheel. My friend Robby Anton swallowed the big one, then lay himself out encircling his body with the cards of the tarot and placing a jewel on his third eye. That had style. Of course, since I'm a nonswimmer, a dramatic plunge into the deep might be fitting for me—after all, I'm a water sign. . . .

See what I mean? I think about it every day and don't know why. Ah well, in one ear and out the other. Then there was that famous existential suicide: On his knees, the poetic fellow breathed chloroform till he passed out and then drowned face down in two inches of water— he went with the flow but there wasn't much depth to it. Then there's the margarita, which I'm told is nothing more than a temporary form of suicide. I guess that will do for now.

"Garçon! Por favor, una margarita straight up, with half salt."

* I've had lots of dancing partners through the years. One pairing that audiences really liked was with Twiggy. Something about our chemistry clicked onstage that went beyond just our obvious physicality. We fit somehow. It's difficult for me to assess our partnership because you must realize I've never seen us perform together. When one is primarily a stage performer one has no sense of what the audience's experience is. One can only feel the moments and hope for the best. Twiggy and I came to feel things in tandem.

*Twiggy was my partner in *My One and Only* and so trusting. Brave girl, brave woman.

*Twiggy got me this job in *The Boy Friend*
film. Great agent. Great gams.

During our extremely successful Broadway run of *My One and Only* we were invited to appear at a Royal Command Performance in London at the Drury Lane Theatre in the presence of Her Majesty Queen Elizabeth II. It meant leaving New York on Sunday evening immediately after our matinee performance, Concorde-ing it to London, rehearsing on Monday afternoon, doing the big show Monday night, and then Concorde-ing it back to New York, arriving just in time for our Tuesday night performance. Whew!

In those days—before Princess Di and Fergie—the royal family was loved and revered. The idea of being "presented at court" was thrilling, and Twiggy was an enthusiastic Royalist. "Oooh! I just *love* the queen and the queen mum, too, in their matching coats and hats. They're so luverly." Her excitement at meeting the queen face to face and knowing that Broadway was the direct route was infectious. I was in a state of bliss. I owe Twiggy a lot. She saw me on *The Gold Diggers* TV show when it ran in England, told Ken Russell that I'd be perfect for *The Boy Friend* film, and I was cast. Her celebrity, which she shared so generously, made it possible for me to meet famous people (Paul McCartney, John Schlesinger, Tony Richardson, Maggie Smith, George Harrison) I'd never have known otherwise. She also bartered us a free transatlantic crossing on the QE II, free clothes for posing in English *Vogue*, and a raft of other privileges I could never have afforded. She also brought a very special brilliance to our *One and Only* Broadway outing.

*Schiavone shot this of us. Twiggy said,
"We don't really look that good."
She's so pragmatic. She can knit, too.
I have a sweater to prove it.

*The water dance from *My One and Only*.
I can't swim, but I'm drawn to the ocean. I
actually choreographed this dance at low
tide in front of my beach house on the Atlantic
Ocean and then transferred it to Broadway.
Twiggy always liked my pins. She called
them, "The best legs in the business."
I never argue with Twiggy.

The Royal Command Performance was to be televised, and Gene Kelly was set to be the master of ceremonies. I was so honored that he would be introducing us as a pair to the queen and to all of England. It was not to be.

The rehearsal was complicated by the fact that the English producers had chosen our "water dance" from *My One and Only*, a nifty routine done in a narrow tank of water two inches deep and stretching the entire width of the proscenium opening. The Drury Lane stage is fully trapped, which means that the water tank was to be loaded on to an elevator in the basement and then raised to the stage level at the appropriate time. We were set to close the first half. The act directly preceding us was done in front of the house curtain—"in one" as we say in show biz parlance—while the stagehands set up our complicated water works behind.

Not everyone was informed of the tricky elevator move that had to occur, and in the haste and excitement of that one-time-only event, a stagehand walked out on the stage in the darkness and fell through the hole, plunging into the tank far below. Twiggy and I were waiting nervously in the wings, and when she saw him fall she let out an uncontrollable, blood-curdling scream. The elevator's ascent was immediately curtailed. In the half light a rescue team climbed down to assess the damage—the rest of the large cast was hovering over the giant opening—a flurry of fear and concern and babble, directions were being shouted, chorus girls were crying, chaos reigned. Out front the queen sat regally in her royal box reviewing the show. The poor per-

* "Howdy, Ma'am." We were told to call
Her Majesty "Ma'am," and not to
speak till spoken to. Her skin glowed.
So does Twiggy's.

former in front carried on valiantly in spite of her being able to hear the furor from behind the curtain. She finished her rendition of "Broadway Baby," and miraculously we were in place. There was a pause and then the audience erupted. In the darkness Twiggy and I, still shaken by the backstage accident, wondered what on earth was happening. Gene Kelly had been set to introduce us, but no, a huge surprise—we heard another voice—a perfect English instrument. It was Sir Laurence Olivier. He'd gotten wind that we were flying over for the big event and asked if he might introduce us to the queen. Wow! Before the jewel-encrusted crowd, he began, "If a young cockney lass from Neasden were to ask 'How do I get to Broadway?' you'd have to say 'you can't get there from here.' But she *did* and has triumphed overwhelmingly with her brilliant partner in a new musical entitled *My One and Only*. Your Majesty, I give you *the hottest thing on four legs*—direct from Broadway, Twiggy and Tommy Tune."

We were on. The curtain rose. The follow spots hit us, and we made a big splash—literally. After the show we met the queen and she really was the *queen*. She does the royal bit extremely well. She was gracious, warm, and very *interested*. She asked if we had jet lag. Charming. She was wearing royal blue velvet with a crown of diamonds and sapphires, necklace, earrings, and bracelets to match. She reminded me of a great ship in full sail. As she pulled into our port Twiggy said to me, under her breath, "Tommy, the jewels she's wearing are *real*." I was agog, and I have a picture of my eyeballs to prove it. I'm probably making another politically incorrect blunder, but I really love the idea of Britain's royal family—the historic quality of it, the pomp and circumstance. I think it's nice to have someone to look up to, and we were both definitely impressed with Her Royal Majesty Queen Elizabeth II. They don't make 'em like that any more.

As for the stagehand who took the plunge, he was crippled for life. It's a downer for the end of this story but once again illustrates the bitter irony of show business vs. reality. The glamour of it all juxtaposes the hard truth. Pause. As Sir Tyrone Guthrie says, "On."

* I danced with Tina Turner once. In the seventies Don Kirshner, who was TV's first rock concert promoter, had hired me to host a television series called *Get Dancin'*. We were set to shoot the weekly series in discothèques all over the world—Amsterdam, Paris, London, Rome, New York, Rio—good job! The idea was we'd have dancing stars from every corner of show business—ballet, jazz, R and B, rock, flamenco, country and western, Broadway, film—as our weekly guests, and they would perform the type of dancing in which they excelled. Rudolph Nureyev and Margot Fonteyn were being pursued, Twyla Tharp and Company, Chita Rivera, Galina Ulanova and other stars of the Bolshoi Ballet, the Stony

Mountain Cloggers, Shirley MacLaine, Fred Astaire, Alicia Alonso, Merce Cunningham, Juliet Prowse, François Czony and Nancy Clare, The Nicholas Brothers, Jose Greco—get the picture? There, in the designated disco scene, these dancing stars would appear, be interviewed, and dance. It sounded like a fun show to me.

Our pilot was to be shot in Los Angeles at the then reigning disco on the West Coast, Studio One. The guests were to be Phyllis Diller (who I taught to Hustle), Ken Berry (who I tap danced with), Chuck Berry (I got to do that fun flea hop step he innovated), Antonia Ellis (my dancing partner from *The Boy Friend* film), and the Ike and Tina Turner Revue. The show's producers were terrified of Ike as was everyone else apparently. Our show was totally scripted, and after Ike and Tina's first number I was to go into a dialogue with Tina wherein I asked her if she would make a dream of mine come true. "Could I please, please, please be an Ikette, if only for one night?" We were well into taping the show, and there was no sign whatsoever of the Ike and Tina Turner Revue. We were all on serious alert.

"The moment they arrive we stop whatever we're shooting and send them on. Otherwise Ike will walk. He'll *walk*."

OK. OK. I was in the middle of a big tap number with the sixteen chorus dancers who had been hired for the show (Tony Mordente was the choreographer/director), when suddenly the plug got pulled. The Ike and Tina

Turner Revue had arrived. One, two, six, and they were on. I'd never met Tina Turner, I'd never heard the song in which I was to become an Ikette, I'd never gone over the lines with her—nothing. By now Ike, Tina, and the Ikettes had whipped the audience into a frenzy. The stage manager threw me out onstage into the middle of that screaming mass.

The script guys were holding up cue cards with our "clever" dialogue all written out, "Hi, Tina, this is so exciting. I was wondering if . . ." Forget it. I'm hurled on, and Tina says, "Hi, Tommy, I hear you wanna be an Ikette. Well, OK." The cards got tossed, and from behind us Ike counted off the new tempo. This amazing energy pumped out from his musicians, propelling us into high action. It was the damnedest sensation. It was like involuntary fornication except from the back. Whooee!

Now I'm between the Ikettes, whose costumes were unbelievably raveled and worn—dirty, in fact. But no matter, I was into the routine, and it was hot. Then Tina pulled me out from the group to "duet" with her. Double wow. I've *never* experienced anything like this. I missed not one step, not a slide, not an arm, not a turn, not a bump. No mistakes. I was perfect. Lucie Arnaz had come to the taping to cheer me on, and afterward she wondered when I'd had time to learn such a complicated routine. I hadn't. When I got back to New York I told Michael Bennett about the magic. He listened, then simply said, "Oh, you were dancing." And that's that.

The pilot of *Get Dancin'* didn't sell, and here's why: I

begged them to shoot it at Studio 54 in New York, which was the center of the world at that time, but for financial reasons they chose Studio One in Los Angeles. Studio One was basically a gay disco but for our evening they'd kept the gays out and invited another social set. Not many of the invited group showed, so in a last-ditch effort to people the vast space, they opened the doors to the waiting regulars, all guys. I was in the control booth for the beginning of the evening and heard a panicked Tony Mordente directing the cameramen to get off *that* couple and try to find a girl somewhere. "Camera six— pick up *that* couple—Oh no, that's just a guy with long hair. Oh, God." Disaster. They couldn't show the excitement on the floor because it was all gay, and they were trying to sell this to the networks. So much for *Get Dancin'*. It's not enough to have a good idea; you have to see it through, detail by detail.

* Another all-time favorite dancing partner of mine, and one whose influence on me was more than major, was that gentleman of gentlemen, Charles "Honi" Coles. It's easy to describe Honi in one word—elegant.

He was part of a vaudeville class act known as Coles and Akins. Their big number was billed as the world's slowest soft-shoe. It was magnificent. The space between the tap sounds was as important as the sounds

*Dancing with Honi Coles, who told me,
"Tommy, be more nonchalant. Never
let them see you working." Good advice.
Hide the toil. I'm working on it, Honi.

themselves—sort of like understanding and appreciating negative space in the composition of a great painting. What's left out is as important as what's shown. I met Honi during the making of *My One and Only;* he was seventy-five at the time, and our title song duet stopped the show every night. He toured with the show after our Broadway run, and it was always a joy to dance in tandem with him each and every performance—except one.

We were playing Grand Rapids, Michigan, on a Saturday matinee. Honi was always a trifle fragile on matinee days—he *did* like his Dewars. We played a comedy scene, which led into our tap number. I was the straight man; Honi had all the laughs. It was a swell scene. This particular performance he couldn't seem to recall his lines, couldn't form his words; it got worse. Finally the stage manager started yelling his lines to him, no dice. It wasn't happening. Jack Lee, our conductor, threw the music cue from the pit. "Honi" brightened and started the song, "My one and only, what am I gonna do if you turn me down . . ." and as if on automatic pilot, we slid into the dance. He accomplished it, perfectly.

The audience responded with enthusiastic applause. I always let him decide if we should do the encore. We *always* did, but not today. Under his breath he said, "I don't think so." He sat down, and the scene ended. He'd had a stroke right there on stage with me. The left half of him never recovered. He never danced again.

A few weeks later from New York he called me,

sounding brave and chipper, "Hey, Tommy, got any work for a one-legged tap dancer?" What a guy. What a dancing partner.

＊ During one of the valleys of "My Brilliant Career," I found myself making an Italian movie playing opposite the then reigning queen of the Italian cinema, Monica Vitti. The movie was entitled *Mimi Bluette, Fiore del Mio Giardino* (Mimi Bluette, Flower of My Garden). It was quite an elaborate epic, set in the early 1900s in Paris. I played a Svengali-like choreographer who had discovered this lowlife waif and out of very raw material saw potential and created one of the great celebrated dancers of the era. She was worshiped by an adoring host of fans, and I, of course, had fallen in love with my creation. She was the toast of Paris, and one night we decide to visit our old haunts: the bars, the brothels, and the cabaret in which her phenomenal career had begun.

The film, based on a very popular novel by a D'Annunzio imitator, was absolutely beautiful to behold. Those amazing Italian craftsmen had created the most extraordinarily authentic art nouveau interiors imaginable—Mimi's elaborate apartments overlooking all of Paris, her backstage dressing rooms, those gaslit bars and cabarets of the demimondaine, etc. The costumes, designed by Corrado Collabucci, were exquisite. I re-

*Looking like something out of an Italian movie.
The truth, in fact. On the set of *Mimi Bluette, Fiore del
Mio Giardino*, filmed in Rome and Paris. By the end of
the shoot, I could speak Italian like a seven year old.
*Bravo. Che bella lingua.*

member volumes of silks and feathers and furs and jewels, exotic and dripping with theatricality as the milieu and time dictated. The whole thing was lovingly and artistically photographed by the director, Carlo Di Palma, who has become Woody Allen's primo cinematographer. Carlo created a beautiful film for the moviegoer's eye.

In the story, on this one delirious night visiting our old terrain, Mimi catches sight of this elusive stranger in the shadows, and in that moment is smitten. He disappears in an instant, and the rest of the film traces her downfall as she desperately searches for him on a trail that leads her eventually through the Sahara Desert and into other exotic locales. My character is insane with jealousy and eventually completely broken by grief as he watches his magnificent creation destroy herself for want of this seductive dream of a man. It was very Italian.

Monica Vitti, who was one of the most beautiful women out of makeup I have ever seen, was compelling. I was dazzled by her beauty, and maybe if I had been able to let that show in my onscreen portrayal, I might have done an acceptable performance. Unfortunately, film is not my medium, and I was pretty bad I'm afraid. I looked great, however, and had been dubbed by an Italian voiceover actor with a remarkable instrument. God, I wish I really sounded like that! But then, everything sounds better in Italian and looks better, too.

Corrado dressed me, for every scene, entirely in pale cream colors—he called me his "butter boy"—and my hair was meticulously coiffed every morning with special curling irons. The makeup man was a genius. He had the lightest touch with his face paints and eye liners that I've ever witnessed, hardly using any makeup from his pallettes. I never looked better in my life. Carlo, our director, certainly understood light and operated the camera himself. The shots were gorgeous.

The acting . . . well, let's just say that the look was really more important in Italian cinema of that time than the acting. The international cast playing scenes in their native tongues were a personified Tower of Babel. The cast included Shelley Winters as Mimi's lower-class mother, a French actor as Mimi's majordomo, a pair of German twins, an African cocaine peddler, and a Spanish flamenco dancer. To observe this lot of us trying to play a quick-paced scene in all of our mother tongues must have been interesting. We had to memorize the last word of whatever language was being spoken, then jump in with our speech. Italian, French, German, Swahili, Spanish, and English ricocheted around the walls of the studio, and the effect was dizzying—and to me, hilarious. Being a complete language cripple as most of us Americans are, I didn't know what the hell was happening. I noticed, however, that Monica had devised an amazing technique. When someone else was speaking other than in her native Italian, she would avert her eyes and busy herself with fixing her costume or her hair, or picking up an interesting prop on the set and scrutinizing it, or catching the eye of someone not speaking and flirting—anything to divert the viewer from the fact that she couldn't understand what the actor speaking was actually saying. Once he came to the word that was her cue, then she would lock into his eyes in perfect stillness and utter her lines. It was amazing. I was in awe. I also had a hard time keeping a straight face. Sometimes show business advances to the ridiculous.

The whole event reached its apex for me when Monica and I, who played lovers, had to shoot our nude scene. NUDE SCENE! I kept nervously laughing about what my parents might think down in Houston, Texas, when the film played there. I needn't have. *Mimi Bluette, Fiore del Mio Giardino* never made the leap across the Atlantic Ocean, and my lengthy nakedness hasn't been seen publicly outside of Italy. Whew!

Dealing in all these disparate languages slowed down filming considerably, and consequently we went way over schedule. We were supposed to be finished by the top of December, but as Christmas approached it was clear that we wouldn't be done. Production shut down for the holidays, and the Italian producers kindly shipped me home to New York for a few days.

I was in a long-standing romantic relationship and was thrilled to be arriving home for Christmas to spend that special time of year with my partner. I hadn't seen Michel for six months, and he was riding high, as a member of the original cast of *A Chorus Line,* which had opened on Broadway while I was in Europe. I had seen the first performance of that amazing show at the Public Theatre where it originated and was eager to celebrate it's phenomenal success now that it had moved to the Shubert Theatre. My heart was absolutely palpitating as the elevator lifted me up to our top-floor loft on 17th Street and Fifth Avenue. As the door opened our 2,500 square feet of open loft space was filled with red poinsettias interspersed with tall glowing candles. It was breathtaking. What a welcome. Michel was there and waiting for me, and I was ecstatic to see him, to be back in New York, to be in our beautiful home. Pause. What's happening? Michel was oddly distant, but I chalked it up to that little period of adjustment that pairs have to go through when they've been separated for a while. We sat down, and he lit a sparkler. It was a magical setting, that field of candles and poinsettias and Michel with the sparkler held high over his head. But I detected something in his eyes—something off—that prompted me to ask, "Michel, what's wrong?"

He answered, "Nothing. I'm in love with someone else."

I was stunned by the timing and bluntness of this pronouncement. It was like a body blow. I headed directly for the shower. Water has always held a great healing power for me. My highest thoughts seem to come in, or on, or near water. There's also a solace that this element provides that's almost nourishing, and I certainly needed nourishment at this moment.

The object of Michel's passion was the brilliant dancer Louis Falco. Louis was truly beautiful and gifted, and I thought as the water poured over me, "So you're in love with Louis Falco. So go ahead and love this Louis Falco. Who am I to say who you should love? This isn't about your loving me or not loving me. It's about my loving you. And I do. If you have to love someone else, that's *your* heart beating. *My* heart is beating for you as it has for the past seven years."

I suddenly felt all right with this perspective, and my breathing seemed to settle into a relaxed pattern. I'd been away from home for six months. I was glad to be back. I had tales from the Italian film industry to share. Rome was hopping at that time: Fellini was filming *Casanova* with Donald Sutherland at Cinecittà; Vincent Minnelli was directing his daughter Liza in *A Matter of Time* with Ingrid Bergman and Charles Boyer at Cine Studi Dear; Visconti was shooting *Innocenti* with Giancarlo Giannini and Laura Antonelli; and Pasolini was creating what was to be his last film, for during my stay in Rome he was brutally murdered, and all of the Italian cinema mourned the loss. Concurrently rumor had it that Liza and Donald Sutherland had locked eyes in the Piazza Navone one hot evening and had disappeared for three days making "the beast with two backs" while production on both their films was curtailed. No one could find them. It was an enormous scandal.

Carlo Di Palma and Monica Vitti were ex-lovers and fought on the set, incessantly. He loved her profile, and she didn't want her profile shot. He was right. Monica had a Roman nose, and her profile was absolutely Patrician. She really was an astounding woman to behold. Round and round they went. I had all these fresh experiences to tell. It was Christmas, and Michel was in love with Louis Falco. Pause. On.

Louis was preparing holiday dinner, and I was invited. Now that's an odd position to be in, I grant you, and I'd never played the cuckold before. I swallowed my pride and showed up, full of the Christmas spirit. A few other guests had arrived, and as I walked into Louis's apartment he excitedly yelped, "Wait! Wait!" and ran to the stereo. He put the needle down on Harry Nilsson's latest album. The cut went:

> I say Jesus
> I say Jesus
> I say Jesus Christ
> You're tall.
> I bet nobody
> I bet nobody
> I bet nobody wants
> to dance with you at all.

That was Louis's sense of humor. *Everyone* laughed, as did I. It was humiliating. Louis served a delicious Italian feast, and with each course divested himself of a layer of his clothing. By the time the pasta course was finished he was shirtless, his torso "bulging with pulsating muscles" as the lyric goes, and it was clear what was being served for dessert that evening and who would be eating it. I paid my compliments and left. Feliz Navidad.

A high-class hooker I once knew in Paris at the Ritz Hotel told me there were such things as "unforgivable hurts," and I always remembered it. Intellectually one can deal with ill treatment when it confronts one, but deep down inside something gets skewed that can never heal over, and if it does heal there's still a scar to remind one of how vulnerable the human heart can be.

I returned to Rome and finished filming *Mimi Bluette*. We did exterior location shooting in Paris. It was like living in a dream. We did a shot on the Pont Neuf. The traffic, pedestrian and motor, of that busy day in Paris had to be halted, then all the horses and carriages and extras in period clothing claimed the bridge. Monica and I would drive through in our open-top, cream-colored horseless carriage playing our scene. Then traffic would be released, and modern-dressed Parisians and our period-dressed extras would comingle as modern-day cars crisscrossed with our antique autos and carriages. It was surreal. Two distinct eras living together in one moment of time.

To me, what happens off camera in the making of a movie is always so much more interesting than what ends up on the screen. Why have one world when you can have two?

Back in Italy my last shot in the filming was in a beautiful forest in the Italian countryside just before sunset. It was part of a flashback sequence when Mimi and I were in love—she was in yards and yards of China silk with extended wands from her arms that made her out to be some kind of ethereal butterfly in the golden sunlight of the late Italian afternoon. We were dancing together, a sort of Nijinsky and Loie Fuller duet. It was poetic and romantic and beautiful. What a contrast to what was actually happening in my secret life. It's amazing how in the depths of hurt the acrobatic heart of an actor can continue to do its tricks. In the last rays of that perfect Italian sunset, Monica and I completed our last shot of the film. I had to run for my plane, which was leaving from the Rome airport in two hours. I knocked on Monica's trailer door to bid her a hasty good-bye. Her red wig had been ripped from her head, her blonde hair cascading down—complete dishabille— one eyelash off, the lifts hanging on either side of her face, a towel wrapped around her breasts. Laughing and crying we bid farewell—I've not seen her since. She was so beautiful. Did you see her in Antonioni's *Red Desert*? If not, do.

By the time I returned to New York I think the great passionate affair between Michel and Louis was beginning to cool. It wasn't discussed but it was obvious that *our* relationship was over. I moved out. A year or so later Michel came to my new apartment in tears and said, "I want to come back. I want us to be together again."

I said, and meant, "Michel, I've found a new life alone

now. I'm seeing people and exchanging ideas and new thoughts and living with myself, and I realize it's really better this way." I'm sorry that I couldn't return to our relationship, but I couldn't. The hooker at the Ritz was right—there really are unforgivable hurts.

With time I'm learning to be more forgiving, but I still have a lot of work to do in that area. I have a very long fuse but once it reaches the dynamite stick, the blast, which is curiously mute, annihilates that part of my world, obliterates that part of my heart. The relationship was blown to smithereens and not a particle of that once true feeling remains. I have to fake civility and kindness and compassion with Michel these days. I'm sure he doesn't understand that. I simply don't have that part of me to give him anymore. It's not that I'm being stubborn by withholding my feelings; my feelings simply don't exist anymore. There's a vacuum there instead. It's sad but true. A portion of me died that night in that field of Christmas flowers and glowing candles. I thought that Michel had arranged that beautiful scene for my homecoming. I was wrong. It was all a Christmas gift from Louis. Feliz Navidad. On.

---

✶ Laurence Olivier once confessed, "I am prepared to believe that the sense of romance in those of our brothers and sisters who incline towards love of their own sex is heightened to a more blazing pitch than in those who think of themselves as 'normal.'" This could be true, but my most complete, passionate, romantic, and sexual relationship to date has been with a female. A very beautiful and very, very famous female. During our relationship in which I was deeply in love and I believe the feeling was mutual, she was named one of the ten most beautiful women in the world. She was so modest and offhand about it. "Oh, it's just because I happen to be in New York, and that's where they're shooting the pictures." So modest, so astonishing, so beautiful. I think I fell in love with her the first time I saw her. It had been years earlier. We were cast in a project together in another country, and when I arrived at the studio direct from the airport, she was already rehearsing. She was dancing in another man's arms. As he dipped her, her hair fell back, revealing her beautiful face, and I thought to myself, "So, this is _____."

I'm going to call her Jane. It was my nickname for her. If you think you know her real name, go ahead and substitute it. The name is not really important. The love that I experienced is. This is a memoir, and I would be leaving out the heart of this book if I didn't include the following reminiscence. Jane had been a worldwide celebrity from the age of fourteen and had handled the fame game with what seemed to be equanimity. She was a working-class girl elevated to goddess stature by a frenetic press, and she had certainly risen to the occasion. When we met, neither of us was available. I was in the exact middle of my multiyeared relationship with Michel, and she was equally enmeshed with a chap she'd known before all the notoriety exploded her name and face across the universe. I think we both felt the undercurrents of attraction, but what were we to do?

Oddly, we were not playing opposite each other in the project at hand, but this inexpressible energy had to come out some way. Here's how: Her actual leading man was a very attractive and tormented and beautiful and married-with-children lead dancer, fresh from a world-class ballet company. Jane developed a crush on him immediately, and he and I developed a crush on each other simultaneously. What a mess! What underpinnings! The three of us were all far away from our partners and became a strange shimmering trio that the rest of the cast must have found quite amusing. People know, you know, and I'm sure they had a lot of laughs figuring out who was doing what and to whom. The married man and I would see Jane to her door each evening and then bolt back to one of our rooms to make the old, or should I say the new, "mad and passionate." For it really was. For a male partner, he was the best I've ever experienced, and it was especially odd for me because the role I was used to playing in a guy/guy pairing had been reversed. It was all new, but inextricably linked to Jane. Somehow since it was a guy thing it didn't seem adulterous at all to us, although technically it was. However, he wasn't cheating on his wife with another woman, and I wasn't doing an unforgivable either by crossing over from my queer relationship and sleeping with a female.

Eventually it had to end, and with the end of the project we three were split asunder. However, the currents between Jane and me, the unexpressed feelings, would eventually become manifest, but not until ten years later. Ten years. Do you think I move too hastily? Do you believe in love at first sight? That once two beings connect visually on a certain level, the inevitable will happen, no matter how unendurably the feeling must be prolonged? I certainly do. I didn't know anything at the time, but looking back—the wisdom of experience, you know—there was no way that Jane and I were not going to fall in love. The force is too strong. It propels the universe. It's what they write the songs about, commit crimes of passion for, fight wars over. It's very unruly and consuming, and God, I wish I were going through it all again, right now! Being truly in love with another human being on this earth is the best thing that can happen to a person. I know because I've experienced it. I experienced it with Jane, and at the height of it all I remember asking her—because she is definitely my emotional superior—"Will it be like this forever?" And she shrugged, "Don't know. How can anyone know?" and it was the perfect answer. It was the truth. She could easily have given me an "in the throes of passion-romantic-poetic" answer, but she didn't. She told me the truth. Remember saying that, Jane? You were the great love of my life, the one that worked on all levels—intellectually, spiritually, artistically, and definitely physically. Wow. I never had it so good. We were one candle burning at both ends.

I've pondered the demise of our romance for years, and I'm not any closer to an answer now than I was as it was happening. The closest I can get is that I was consumed, not by her, but by "it," the intimacy, the drowning sensation, the loss of self. Perhaps that is when the jealous lover within—the artist—rises up and says, "What about me? When are you going to take the materials out of the bin and create *me* on canvas? Why are you giving all your love to *her* and not to *me?*" Who was speaking? Another me? I don't know. I know that to give love is to receive love, and one equals the other. But maybe my way of loving is alien to this world and not meant to be expressed in the "normal way." I don't know this beast within but he demands his creation, and maybe that's simply my gift or curse or my mode of repaying the world for the privilege of being here. Anyway our romance ended at the elevator on Halloween. Jane had gone to the party as Vampira and I as a skeleton. Blood dripped down from her mouth and tears slid down her beautiful face as she pressed the up button, and the doors closed on our intimate time together, forever.

Jane, it was you. Thank you for showing me what it can be.

Now that I've flipped both sides of my sexual coin for you, I'd like to share an observation that I've never thought about before. It seems that to be the complete sexual being, one has to experience the loss of virginity twice. Once in the "normal" way in which I suppose the procreating instinct more or less leads you, and then in the other more complicated and subtle way in which you have to intuit directly from your partner what's appropriate, what's desired, what's needed, what's appealing. The latter is more difficult because you don't have the wisdom of the ages to guide you. In fact, you have taboos and feelings of guilt stopping you, and yet there is an overpowering energy force to share yourself with that particular individual. Yet you are the same, and what a mystery it is! To find love and intellectual stimulation and similarities and dislikes and dual tastes, with enough differences to keep it all interesting, and perfect physical couplings that match and attract is a crapshoot. Given the odds, it's a miracle that *any* kind of pairing is successful.

But the main thing in life, I'm convinced, is to find that other one, that other half of you, and then do everything possible to make it stick and last and hold and remain and endure and change and thrive and grow. I am still on the quest. Undeterred. Aware. I'm not suggesting that the double initiation is *the* way, the flipping of both sides of the sexual penny. It's simply *a* way. Being raised Christian suggested to me that such experimentation was wrong, but I am a good person, an imperfect person, a God-loving person, and when a force as strong as this quest for a partner overtakes me and I know that my motive first and last and always is to love in all the aspects available to us human beings, then I can't condemn myself in terms of Christian dogma. I do not go about hurting other people. I only seek to share my existence with others. It's their prerogative to walk away or embrace me. Some have walked away, some have stayed for the embrace. You can't win 'em all.

When I was in junior high school I was coming out of the auditorium after a rehearsal, carrying my tap shoes, and a group of hoods called me a "queer." I didn't know what it meant so I went to the school library, opened the giant dictionary on the wooden lectern, and looked it up. I guess other kids had wanted to know what it meant, too, because, holy cow, where the word "queer" was printed the page had been worn through. There was just a hole. I skipped down to "queerer," which was, I thought, close enough. It read: "Queerer: one who queers." I laughed out loud. And I'm still laughing.

I'm a bisexual; I have sex twice a year.

—Anonymous

I'm simply a combination of everything I've ever seen or heard or read or done. And maybe one part more— my "blood memory" as Martha Graham calls it: all those molecular remembrances with which I arrived on this planet, all those tiny dots of matter, present from birth, dating back to and inherited from my Indian and

*A Lone Star state. On the pinnacle of my
beach house with the Texas flag. Jack Vartoogian
took this photo, and it won a contest.
Thanks, Jack.

English ancestors through their direct blood lines or perhaps even before. So here I stand, part Brit, part Shawnee, and as my friend Todd Ruff says, "with good taste and mixed blood," introduced to sex by an older woman in East Texas, deflowered by a Black ballerino in the Midwest, and spinning constantly to forgive myself for all the foolishness I've practiced—still seeking some still center from which to proceed. As I see it, we're all dealt a hand in this life, and I got some unusual cards. I'm not a good bluffer; I play the cards I'm dealt. The traditional sex card is a great card. I didn't get it. Deal me another. OK. Deal me another. Oh, that, too. Let's play. Some people consider such a hand of cards an unfair handicap. It's not really. There's pain involved, but then with every play of the cards the game changes anyway. Moment to moment.

I just want to live in my time.

Maria McKenna believes that, "We are all physically descended from stardust. After the Big Bang there remained only stardust, and those particles settled into the primordial soup. Out of the primordial soup emerged the first cell. We all have a piece of that first cell within us. We are all fiftieth cousins once removed." Comforting, ain't it? Makes me wonder why there is a racist or a sexist on the planet. We're all the same. Descended from stardust.

After Jane, I became involved in a "rebound" relationship that somehow clung on to become a longtime thing. By the very virtue of loving me and just being there, David insinuated himself into being a hugely important part of my life. Once I asked him flat out why he was here with me, and he said he'd early on asked himself the same question and had answered to himself, "David, go with this man and you'll never be bored." I think I lived up to at least that part of his expectations, if for no other reason than we were too busy to ever be bored. He'd been a ballet dancer before an accident curtailed his career. When we came together he was working as a waiter and doubling as a fitness instructor. Before I knew it he'd moved in with me and had become a full-fledged stage manager on our world tour of *My One and Only*. No one called the show better than David. Being a dancer by root, rhythm and movement were in his blood. He had the knack to make a set arrive on the beat and call a light cue so it brightened simultaneously with the arrival of the set and precisely on that accent in the orchestra—neat. Rare. This is an exacting science and requires expert timing, nerves of steel, and remarkable communicative skills with the operating crew. David had all three plus a sunny disposition that everyone just loved. He was intensely loyal and protective and was determined above and beyond the call of duty or love to make everything just right for me. The only thing he withheld from me was himself.

David was addicted to alcohol and cocaine and cigarettes. When you live with an alcoholic you don't realize it in the beginning. In fact, although David was always addicted to diet pills and downers, I didn't realize he was a full-fledged alcoholic until after we were in the midst of our relationship. Maybe I caused it or provided for it, but through the years, as tender as our relationship was, he became more and more remote from me. The more important he became in my career, the further into himself he retreated. When we were alone, he ended up spending hours in his bathroom to avoid conversation. This will tell you something: We never had a fight. Ten years together, and we never had a fight. That's not normal, but there was really nothing normal about David or our relationship.

He was sweet and kind and funny, and it was all a performance covering I know not what. He came from the Midwest and was good at making people laugh. He could also throw a swell party, and the one he arranged for my fiftieth birthday was a corker. He covered the entire ceiling of the penthouse in white balloons spelling out Tommy in black balloons and then projecting my name in light over and over and over again on all the walls. He was also very clever with his hands. He had cut out the letters of my name in heavy aluminum foil and placed these slides over theatrical lights, which he rigged all over the apartment. The time and the care that went into it was astounding, but I would have preferred just to have had that time with him. *That* he couldn't share.

One day there was a knock on the door. I loped across the living room to open it. There stood little David with a grin on his face and looking like the cat that ate the canary. I'm thinking, "He has a key, why doesn't he use it? What's going on?"

Behind him in the hallway I see a little fur ball of a critter crawling along between the carpet's edge and the wall. I get down on my knees and lift it up in my hands. It's a tiny baby Yorkshire terrier. David had spent the day with him in a pet store making the decision and then brought him home for us. Now, usually couples discuss having a child before they conceive, and I would think the same might hold true in bringing a third living party home to roost. Not so with David, and yet it was the best thing he ever did. I'd never had a dog before; we had horses down home. Suddenly I was a dog parent, and Ophie has become the center of my life. He weighs five pounds fully grown, but he thinks he weighs five hundred. He has a huge presence and a strong will and couldn't care less that I've won nine Tony Awards and am trying to finish this book before I'm eighty. He wants to play, and he wants to play now! Excuse me.

*Footnotes* resumed ten minutes later:

Ophie really became our child, and for a short moment I thought that he would be the salvation of our relationship. Not so. David's addictions caused him to send out a lot of mixed signals to Ophie, then an impressionable youngster, so his house training is, shall we say, at best, impressionistic! There're a lot of blurred areas in the discipline department and a lot of carpet stains. I care, but not that much. Ophie has taught me a huge lesson in unconditional love, and I believe that David was sent to me for the same reason.

It was not until Patrick, who is a member of AA, told me I was a "King" enabler that I got the clarion call—David needed serious help. You see, David was never belligerent or staggering, or loud, or unruly, or anything that I had come to believe an alcoholic to be, and living with him from day to day I never saw his condition worsen. He'd arise in the late morning and disappear for a couple of hours into his bathroom, emerge intact, and set about the business of the day, which included lots of paperwork and phone calls. Once, innocently, I picked up his morning coffee mug thinking it was mine, and before he could grab it from me I'd taken a sip. It looked like coffee, but it was vodka and Coke. I didn't know anything about the cocaine addiction till much later. He told me the fact that he couldn't breathe through his nostrils was a "sinus condition," and I had no reason to doubt him. The cigarettes were a constant as with most ballet dancers. So he had all three addictions going on inside of him simultaneously and something else as well.

I had met David on an elevator years before when we were both working the Kenley summer stock circuit. Mr. John Kenley had three hugely successful theaters making a grand triangle within the state of Ohio. There were always three shows going on, and each company traveled the triangle. David was in the outgoing company, and I was coming in. We'd be in the same city for approximately six hours, and we hit it off immediately. When his troupe closed their final show he would borrow the family car and come visit me in whatever city our troupe was playing. He was sweet and fun-loving, and we would just laugh and laugh all through the nights. He'd sneak out of my hotel room in the early morning so I wouldn't have to pay double—in show business it's called "ghosting" and can save a lot of money, single occupancy rates being significantly lower than double. The summer ended, and he went back to his ballet company while I went back to New York. He'd cross my mind occasionally, but we never corresponded. One night nearing the end of the *My One and Only* run on Broadway, Baayork Lee brought him round to my dressing room. She'd met him in fitness class. David and I were both free so we picked up where we left off. The timing and geography were right. The truth is, I was aching inside, and I think he needed someone, too.

It started off great, then one night he made a serious confession to me, which I didn't take for serious at the time. Now as I look back . . . He told me that in the ballet company every Monday morning each dancer had to weigh in, and if they were over, they were out. David loved to dance and was not naturally slim. He existed on diet pills and lettuce. He'd take a whole head of lettuce in his hand and eat it like an apple. That was dinner. So in the ballet company he became hooked on diet pills and was never substance-free again.

In the eighties we were playing Pittsburgh with *Tommy Tune Tonite!*, my one-man show plus thirty. By this time in our lives together David was managing the whole shebang. Jules Fisher and Peggy Eisenhauer had designed the lighting and Tony Walton the set. It was a lot to transport, set up, and run for each performance, and deconstruct, load, and haul from stop to stop, and, to be fair, a lot of that pressure fell directly on David's head. He handled it all, but balancing it were extra doses of his addictive substances.

I was really worried about him, and I couldn't get him to talk about it, couldn't break through the chemical haze. His parents and best girlfriend had come to see the show, and afterward at a private gathering I steeled myself with a shot of tequila, seized the moment, and pounced. I didn't think that in the face of that formidable company he'd be able to retreat into the secret noncommunicado mode he always affected when we were alone. I was desperate. I confronted him in front of his parents urging him to seek professional help. Luckily they concurred with me, as did his girlfriend. We passed the ball to him. Trembling, I awaited his reaction.

He paused and calmly said, "Okay, I'll *go*. On the hiatus."

I breathed again and embraced him. I was so proud of him, of his acceptance, of his understanding that it all came from love. Mid-tour we had a six-week break and off he went to the desert to detox, to dry out, to regroup.

He returned a new man. I was very impressed, and he looked like a million dollars; all the puffiness in his face, the bleary eyes, the clogged breathing, all the symptoms of overindulgence were gone. He'd lost weight and seemed calmer than I'd seen him in years.

To celebrate we had an actual date after the show. We dressed up and went to the finest restaurant in San Diego. During a magnificent dinner I asked him if there was anything he wanted to tell me about his stay in the desert.

He said, "Yes, I was tested. I found out I have AIDS."

Two weeks later he slipped off the wagon, and a year later he was dead.

Following are a couple of entries from my journal documenting our last days together.

December 12, 1994

Today they're taking David off the dialysis machine. He has T.B., pneumonia, thrush, kidney failure—"But his heart is still strong." Of course his heart is strong. He has one of the biggest hearts in Christendom. He is going on and going at the same time. I prayed this morning to God to give him peace. Is that the wrong prayer? I pray to see him released from the suffering. I must call John Lucas to check on *his* health. The line is busy. David's sister Lisa is a champ with him and his mom and dad are present and loving.

The first day in the hospital David was still with

it. I asked him if Liliane could visit him and he shot back—gasping for air but snappy, "Only if she brings me a present," (huge laughs) and then he muttered, "She ignores me all my life and then wants to visit me on my death bed." Six hours later when I returned he couldn't talk and was in and out of consciousness. Now today—both times—he's more so—less and less conscious.

John Lucas's phone is still busy. Fran is due in from London, Gracey is due in from Texas, this mix of Christmas and joy and love and sorrow and suffering is so volatile in my center—one minute I laugh, the next I sob. David's brother and his wife as I write this are having a baby—induced labor because she's ten days overdue—what irony—is it an exchange of souls?

It's almost too dramatic, as life always is. We have to tone it down for the stage. It's too incredulous. Life is like a parody of itself. When it became too much for Andy Warhol he always "turned it into a movie." Thus he could feel like he was looking at it instead of experiencing it. I must get wash cloths and towels for David's parents, Russ and Connie.

December 24, 1994
Last words: As I was leaving his room I said, "David, I love you." He answered, tubes in every orifice, "Ah lawh yaw." Oh God, bring him peace.

December 25, 1994

On December 25th, 1994, David died at 4:00 A.M. Thank you, God, for answering my prayer. Thank you, David, for sharing your life with me. I am a better man because of you. I can't believe you're gone—perhaps you're not. I love you. David, I love you—Merry Christmas. Liliane just called to tell me her old friend Paul Sorel called her this morning—this sad and happy Christmas morning—to tell her he saw a rainbow over Manhattan. We never see rainbows over Manhattan. This is an exceptional day. I can still hear him, "Ah lawh yaw."

December 27, 1994

I want to remember my last real time with David before it fades. Pack rat that he was, we had accumulated stuff in storage lockers all over New York City. It was all gathered together downstairs and after not seeing him for weeks and weeks, in this "warehouse"-like environment we met. He looked as great as he had ever looked—tanned, rested, slightly thinner, trim in fact. The sun was blasting in on the 32nd floor—a perfect day and we went through every box, carton, and trunk—clothing through the years—a veritable fashion retrospective of our times together. We laughed and laughed that we'd ever worn such shit. "How could you have let me out of the house in this?" And then there was

*David Wolfe, then and then. That kiddo's smile never left him throughout his short life. In researching photos for this book, I discovered this one that Martha Swope snapped on the *Grand Hotel* set. A complete surprise. I'd never seen it. It took my breath away. Thanks, Martha.

his formidable collection of "cowboy kitsch"—accumulated for his "cowboy cabin"—an unrealized dream cottage—his peculiar taxidermy collection of critters—moose heads, buffalo heads, deer heads, a stuffed baby bear, giraffe skins, bear skins, fur pelts . . . we joked that the cowboy cabin would have to be a *lodge* to house all this stuff. It was a joyful day and then I had to fly out of town somewhere so I left him still going through it—"To be continued," I said and meant it. It never was. How could I know at the time it was our "last dance."

January 1, 1995

My last gift to David was a tree. His last artistic act was to fill it with lights. The last time I saw him move was when he got out of bed to plug in the lights, smiling, giggling, proudly showing me his creation. And what a creation he was. I loved David Wolfe very much.

Received this letter from David's father, Russ, today:

April 26, 1996

Garfield Hts, OH

Dear Tommy:

I tried calling you, but I know you were very busy. I hope your last trip was a success. And I do hope that your leg is back in shape so as you can again go onstage better than ever.

227

Enclosed is a copy of one of David's accounts, IRA. This account is yours as you are the beneficiary.

This may [sic] of what David wanted you to have, because of the trouble he gave you. And the expense you went through to try and help him. I know he loved you very much and you of him.

Tommy, I still cry when I think of him not only at Xmas but all the time. And I'm sure this is what caused Connie [his mom] to pass away so quickly.

I just paid David's 1994 Income Tax—$4,600.00. And I still have a few more bills to be paid before I can get the remains of his estate. I sold all of his animal skins, except the fur coat. If you want to send some of your inheritance back to me, I would appreciate it. If not I understand your situation.

I still love you Tommie.

Russ

My answering letter:

Dear Russell—

Your sweet letter just made me cry & cry. I miss him so much and to think that he was trying to repay me just breaks my heart because he brought such love and kindness into my life. No amount of money could ever replace that. Now Russell, I want you to have every cent of the money that David left for me. The fact that he cared for me enough to leave me these amounts is just plain overwhelming, and, the residual emotion for David I have, I will carry with me for the rest of my life. Thank you for writing me. You are such a fine man and father. Give my embrace to the rest of the family. How's that new baby? Over a year old, it's hard to believe. Keep in touch and especially give Aunt Verna my love.

Tommy

* This whole thing has gotten kind of heavy hasn't it? Someone once said that our happiness is in direct ratio to the sorrow we've endured. One informs the other. So we go about our days and nights—our busy days and lonely nights, our lonely days and busy nights—which is preferable? I don't know.

This lonely morning I am feeling the loss of David intensely and the loss of Eric Schepard, my late agent who shepherded my career to heights I never imagined possible. He was always there, supporting steadily from beneath and urging me higher up the mountain. With his guidance I won nine Tony awards. Since AIDS claimed his life I've won nothing. My career has foundered. The man behind the man. Gone. And the other man behind the man, David, also claimed by this plague. How my heart has shrunk without him to love. My mother, my father are gone. I'm a fifty-seven-year-old orphan for Godsakes, experiencing a period of severe uncertainty. It's not a surprise to me, but difficult to face each day. Also gone is a vast collection of lifetime friends and colleagues that could fill a page of this book—three columns, single-spaced, most of them younger than me. Gone. I feel like I know nothing, but at least I know this: Acknowledging that you know nothing somehow feels like the beginning of knowledge. So I'm sitting here writing this history of my life.

Somebody said, "It is better to travel hopefully than to arrive."

My bags are packed. I'm ready.

These footnotes are most certainly incomplete. Missing are all the juicy stories of the stars I've worked with. ROLL CREDITS: Peggy Lee, Lillian Gish, Mary Martin, Morgana King, Howard Keel, Betty Hutton, Edward Everett Horton, Gregory Hines, Perry Como, Martha Raye, Jaye P. Morgan, Barbara Cook, Margaret Whiting, Ozzie and Harriet, Raquel Welch, Lauren Bacall, Dean Martin and Jerry Lewis, Britt Ekland, Orson Welles, Phyllis Diller, Patrice Munsel, Joan Rivers, Johnny Carson, Stephanie Powers, Richard Chamberlain, Mae West, Angela Lansbury, Dom DeLuise, Michele Lee, Placido Domingo, David Frost, Chita Rivera, Bernadette Peters, Dinah Shore, Eva Gabor, Merv Griffin, Rosie O'Donnell, Lainie Kazan, Van Johnson, Jay Leno,

Zero Mostel, Marge Champion, Drew Barrymore—the list goes on . . . and expands to include directors, choreographers, designers, photographers, writers, composers, producers—David Merrick, Dore Schary, Gene Saks, Francesco Scavullo, Christopher Isherwood, Paul Morrissey, Joe Kipness, Studs Terkel, Ed Sullivan, Earl Wilson, Richard Avedon, Carol Hall, Dorothy Fields, Greg Gorman, Peter Masterson, Larry King, Fred Ebb and John Kander, Graciela Daniele, Alan Johnson, Peter Gennaro, Zoya Leporska, Michael Kidd, George Abbott, Marty Richards and Mary Leah Johnson, Tad Tadlock, Lee Theodore, Ron Field, Bob Herget, Howard Dietz and Arthur Schwartz, Kevin Kelly, John Arnone, Stevie Phillips, Giorgio Sant' Angelo, Willa Kim, Carmen Schiavone, Fran and Barry Weissler, Shirley and Ken Russell, Harold Prince, Wally Harper—

Stories, stories, omissions, omissions . . .

I've left out so much. If you're interested I could write more.

---

* Tomorrow I turn in these footnotes* to the editors Michael Korda and Chuck Adams of Simon & Schuster for publication. I've just now reread them and find that I've changed my perception on a lot of the issues, and

I'm remembering that's what Marianne calls "a miracle." We're all constantly evolving, and to be a human is to change your mind. Specifically, I've brightened my outlook on my chosen field—the Broadway musical. I just attended the world premiere for a show that's headed to 42nd Street called *Ragtime*, and I really loved it. It's everything a musical should be. I feel that all of our show business history has culminated in this latest theatrical event. I was warmed and inspired to know that such a great musical can be created in this time-span. I urge you to see it. And if I ever get to do another musical, please come see it, too. I promise you that I will have given it my all. OK? Deal? Get out there and support your native American art form!

Work aside, I've also realized that personal incidents that have weighed heavily on me throughout my lifetime don't seem very important right now. In fact, nothing seems very important to me right now except one thing—kindness. Simple basic kindness, whether it's toward the cab driver who answers your hail and takes you to your destination, or toward your nearest neighbor by not playing your music too loudly, or to a friend by quietly understanding and responding to their silent cry for solace, or to an ex-lover by just forgiving him or her for hurting you, or to your dog by making sure he has fresh water before you go out on the town for the evening. Kindness is really important to me right now. Isn't that corny? And yet one of our greatest songwriters, Irving Berlin, said, "There is an element of truth in any idea that lasts long enough to be called corny." I hope kindness lasts. It's the corniest of all.

* These days I fill my time with meetings on forthcoming projects, cooking dinners for friends, going to see choice pieces of theater, being a good audience, writing letters—which seems anachronistic in these computerized times—and playing and sleeping with Ophie. Also I've just completed my first solo album for RCA called *Slow Dancin'*, which is due out soon. I'm still painting when the phone isn't ringing too much; working out with Matt Grace, a fierce new physical trainer who elevates the work to an art form; going to galleries and museums; and doing benefits—OY! I'm looking for love, and I'm looking for an ending to this book. For now, how's this for a finale?

Three of my favorite works, Woody Allen's *Crimes and Misdemeanors*, Tom Stoppard's *Arcadia*, and Michael Bennett's *A Chorus Line*, each end with a dance. The creators of these works seem to be saying, "When the words and thoughts run out, when in doubt, dance." It's always worked for me. Shall we? Let's imagine a waltz. One accented beat, two unaccented beats. Something vaguely Viennese. Read this in rhythm—tempo measured and steady. DON'T RUSH. NEVER RUSH.

Right foot ready and—

One     2     3

          one     2     3

                    one     2     3

               one     2     3

       slow     quick     quick

slow     quick     quick

       right     2     3

               left     2     3

                    turn     2     3

                        turn     2     3

                   front     2     3

       on     2     3

moving     2     3

    turning     2     3

waltzing    2    3

     circling    2    3

              loving    2    3

                   laughing    2    3

              crying    2    3

     dying    2    3

dancing . . .




                  till the tune ends.